HOW TO LEAD TEAMS
AND INFLUENCE PEOPLE

BOSS
LEADER

A GUIDEBOOK TO SUCCESS
FOR THE EMPOWERED BUSINESS
MANAGER OR ENTREPRENEUR

SERENA ELLISON

Table of Contents

Get the Worksheet

Hi, Serena here. I'd just like to say thank you for your interest in my work. Also, I've created a little companion worksheet to help with your journey. We'll be referring to this worksheet in Chapter 3. But download it now so you'll be ready.

If you're reading this book on a Kindle or an iPad, you can click the link below. Or, paperback readers can type the link into your iPhone or PC. Thanks! - Serena

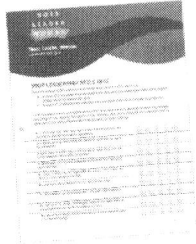

www.tiny.cc/bossleader

Introduction

Women are on the move! The 21st century is a wonderful time to be a woman in the workplace. Though many unique challenges lie before us, many doorways of opportunity have been nudged ajar, waiting for us to push them wide open and step into the corridors of power that have been traditionally occupied by men. Every day, we are witness to a great paradigm shift. The world of business is changing. Women now have the ability to shape the narratives of our industries in ways that our predecessors could have only dreamed of. Thanks to them, we stand on the shoulders of giants. The women who came before us fought hard battles, busted through glass ceilings, and laid the groundwork on which we can now construct a towering edifice of progress and empowerment.

Take a moment to think of the women of history whose leadership qualities you admire. You might consider figures like:

- Eleanor Roosevelt: The trailblazing First Lady who championed civil rights, women's rights, and social justice for all.
- Harriet Tubman: The heroic abolitionist and conductor of the *Underground Railroad* who risked her life to lead enslaved people to freedom.
- Susan B. Anthony: The pioneering activist who fought tirelessly for women's suffrage, ultimately contributing to

the passage of the 19th Amendment, which granted women the right to vote.

In more recent decades, several prominent female business leaders took center stage, including:

- Marillyn Hewson: The former CEO of Lockheed Martin
- Sheryl Sandberg: The former COO of Facebook
- Meg Whitman: The former CEO of Hewlett-Packard

And now, at time of publication, women continue to lead the way with examples like:

- Mary Barra: the Chairman and CEO of General Motors
- Safra Catz: the CEO of Oracle Corporation
- Susan Wojcicki: the CEO of YouTube

According to Morgan Stanley's 2019 report on the rise of the women-led economy (the "SHEconomy" as they termed it), women are already outpacing men in the workforce in some U.S. cities. And the meteoric rise of female-led workspaces is expected to continue. They write:

Today, women make up nearly 25% of the U.S. Congress, compared to just 2% in 1970. In the business world, more women than ever are serving as CEOs [and] board members... Since 2010, the percentage of women executives increased across all developed regions. [Participation rates in American and Europe are up 15% since 2010.] ... A growing body of research demonstrates that gender-diverse firms benefit from the experiences and insights that

norms, new technologies, and a newly diverse labor force creates a dynamic playing field on which the multifaceted proficiencies of women can finally thrive.

Indeed, this is our time to thrive.

This is our opportunity to step up and be heard.

This is our moment to lead.

Ch. 1: What makes a great leader?

What was your first mentor like?

Recall the most influential teachers, coaches, bosses, or mentors that have helped to shape your life.

- What were they like?
- How did they treat the people around them?
- What were the unique traits that made them a good leader?

The more you ponder such questions, the more ethereal their characteristics may seem. If we all knew the exact set of traits that enabled someone to excel at a leadership position, then the process that mega-corporations take when hiring a new CEO wouldn't be so arduous. But since these properties remain ethereal, there's a lot of guesswork involved. It can be beneficial to consider what "the right stuff" might look like. When reflecting on such questions, you may note that the best leaders you've ever known were not the smartest nor the most skilled individuals in the room. Instead, effective leaders possess a unique set of traits that transcend mere intellect.

The Harvard-trained American psychologist Daniel Goleman has been trying to discover the ingredients of this recipe for a long time. In his book *Emotional Intelligence: Why It Can Matter More*

Than IQ, Goleman posits that individuals endowed with a high degree of *emotional intelligence* (what he termed "EQ") are better equipped to navigate complex social situations, manage relationships, and motivate people to action. And since each of these traits is the hallmark of a great leader, it's possible that *emotional intelligence* is more valuable to achieving management objectives than talent, skill, or intellect.

Someone who possesses a high caliber of emotional intelligence is said to have the following three proficiencies in abundance:

1. The ability to monitor and control one's own emotions.
2. The ability to recognize different types of emotions in other people.
3. The ability to utilize emotional information to guide one's thinking and behaviors.

In his famous 1998 article in the Harvard Business Review entitled "What Makes a Leader," Goleman highlighted five traits (or "components" as he called them) of emotionally intelligent leaders. They are:

1. Self-awareness
2. Self-regulation
3. Motivation
4. Empathy
5. Social skill

Let's discuss each component now.

Goleman's Five Components of Leadership

Component 1: Self-Awareness

Goleman's first leadership component, *self-awareness*, refers to the boss's ability to recognize and understand her own emotions, strengths, weaknesses, values, and motivations. A self-aware leader is an introspective leader. She is aware of her whims but not a slave to them. Her ability to adequately manage her emotions enables her to make decisions based on reason and evidence, not *flights of fancy*. Self-awareness can run parallel with humility because it's about having an accurate understanding of your strengths as well as your limitations.

- It's about knowing yourself well enough to be able to admit where your weaknesses lie, all while simultaneously knowing how to capitalize upon your strengths.
- It's about being able to identify what you're feeling in the moment, and having the foresight to predict which stimulus is likely to trigger you.
- It means knowing *who you are* and what drives you.

The best way I've found to improve my own level of self-awareness is to keep a daily log of my most pivotal workplace interactions. No, I'm not talking about writing in a diary. My log is more like an "operation manual for my mind." Just as the technician who fixes your copy machine keeps a dated list of all the issues and repairs that the machine has undergone, so too should you keep a similar record of your lapses in judgment.

- Were you late to arrive at your last meeting? What were the events that caused the tardiness?

- Did you have a fight with a colleague? How might the discussion go better next time?
- Was your team unable to understand your directions during the morning meeting? What could you have said to make the discourse more productive?

These are the sorts of interactions you should be taking note of as you go about your day. Your journal is merely a record of the work-related events and encounters that went well and those that could have gone better. Of course, you need not feel obliged to write a novel. Just jot down the date, a few words of context about the event, and a description of why things went the way they did. After keeping your log for a while, you will begin to recognize patterns in your behavior. And the areas of your life that need improvement will come into focus. In time, you'll develop a better understanding of the triggers that prompt you to react erratically. And you'll be able to assuage such agitating events before they're allowed to boil over. In other words, you'll be in a better position to manifest Goleman's first component: "self-awareness."

Component 2: Self-Regulation

The second component on Daniel Goleman's list is *self-regulation*, sometimes referred to as self-management. It describes one's ability to control one's emotional impulses, as well as the wherewithal to adapt quickly to changing circumstances. The ability to maintain a sense of calm and focus during stressful situations has obvious benefits for anyone in a management position. As a leader, we need to be able to foster a safe work environment—one in which *trust* is high and *in-fighting* is low. Obviously, if the boss is unable to control her own emotions, then employees must contend with both the rigors of work and the volatility of the boss's mood. This is not good for business.

Change is inevitable. The chaotic exigencies of the workday will forever be pelting your peace of mind. And yet, the chore of leadership calls upon us to be the one who remains calm, even while everyone else is in a state of hysterics. If you can manage your emotions and approach obstacles with a clear mindset, then your disposition will be contagious.

Component 3: Social Skill

The third component, *social skill*, refers to the leader's ability to manage workplace relations, build networks of like-minded peers, and navigate complex psychological situations in pursuit of business objectives. Leaders with strong social skills have a keen ability to influence, motivate, or build rapport with staff or colleagues. They are skilled communicators, able to convey their ideas persuasively and tactfully mediate tense situations when conflict resolution or negotiation is called for.

All labor forces consist of people. And people are not mere cogs in a clockwork. They are social animals that come packaged together with the brilliance to innovate and solve complex problems, along with an emotional potpourri of personal biases and incoherent impulses. Your ability to navigate this chaotic milieu is pivotal if you hope to promote a thriving work environment and drive organizational success.

Component 4: Empathy

The fourth component, *empathy*, refers to the leader's ability to understand the emotional state of her employees, particularly when making decisions or delegating tasks. An empathetic leader is able to connect with others on a deeper level, cultivate positive relationships with coworkers, and create a mutually supportive work environment.

Your ability to empathize is the mirror opposite of your ability to be self-aware.

- A *self-aware person* is familiar with the *modus operandi* of her own mind.
- An *emphatic person* is familiar with the *modus operandi* of the mind of everyone else.

To *empathize* is to commiserate with an individual and work toward understanding their viewpoint. When an employee approaches you with a concern, it's important that you not only listen to their claim, but that you genuinely seek to understand their perspective on the matter. By doing this, you can build a stronger bond of trust and respect with the individual, and provide more effective solutions, given that you are aware of the full spectrum of the problem.

Empathy also allows a leader to accurately gauge the impact of their decisions on their team. By understanding how certain decisions may affect the emotions and perspectives of team members, leaders can make more informed, balanced, and considerate choices. Moreover, being empathetic allows leaders to be more in tune with the dynamics of their team. They can identify potential issues or conflicts before they escalate and can take proactive measures to mitigate such obstacles.

Component 5: Motivation

Effective leaders are *motivated* leaders. They seem to possess an innate drive that propels them to excel in their field. But they're usually not driven by a need for reward or recognition. Instead, their desire to succeed seems to come from an *intrinsic* source. This deep commitment to their work naturally results in an enthusiastic and energetic mindset, which can be quite contagious. Employees who have an opportunity to observe their leader's dedication are more likely to mimic her outlook and contribute to the pursuit of her endeavors.

We should take a moment to note the difference between *intrinsic* and *extrinsic* motivation.

- If the boss is only able to compel her labor force to do their job because of external forces—like the promise of a big paycheck or the threat of a swift censure—then her staff is merely spurred to action via *extrinsic* motivators.
- However, if the staff is driven by the spark of internal desire—like the pursuit of mastery, the thrill of victory, or the satisfaction of completing a new goal—then their efforts are fueled by *intrinsic* motivators.

It is your job to discover the ingredients of the *intrinsic motivation elixir* that will be most effective in igniting the passions that drive real business innovation. By discovering and tapping into your team's intrinsic motivators, you can create an environment in which each employee is driven by her unique passions. The sense of fulfillment that arises from such a mindset not only fosters personal growth and satisfaction, it also contributes to the formation of a high-performing and resilient team.

Additional Leadership Traits

While Daniel Goleman's five foundational leadership components are informative, they only provide us with a rough sketch of a complete leadership framework. Expanding upon Goleman's list, let's delve deeper into each leadership trait and identify some additional components. The following list should help to illuminate a more comprehensive picture of effective leadership.

Trait 1: A Clear Vision

When asked, most business leaders will be quick to espouse the value of having a corporate vision—a roadmap that outlines the future trajectory of the organization. However, merely having a vision is not enough. It's ok to be a *visionary*. But it's better to be an *effective visionary*. This calls for at least four components:

1. A definitive goal.
2. A plan to attain the goal.
3. An ability to communicate the goal to others.
4. And a team that possesses both the wherewithal and the confidence to pursue the goal with you.

Of course, during the journey of your career, each of these properties will evolve and change. Goalposts move, strategic plans are discarded, and team members move on to other ventures. Such is the natural order of business evolution. And yet, as the leader, you are the standard bearer that must forever strive to reassess, adapt, and inspire others to action—regardless of the shifting sands that comprise the path to success. Your unwavering dedication to a lofty goal, combined with your ability to navigate the ever-changing landscape that lies before it, instills confidence in your team—fostering the resilience they'll need when times get tough, and the road ahead becomes unclear.

Trait 2: Relationship-building Skills

All leaders need followers. The relationships you build with your staff, customers, and colleagues comprise the support rigging that will hold your wagon train together as you all venture toward El Dorado. An effective leader understands that each relationship has its unique dynamics and requires a personalized approach.

- For customers, this might entail making an effort to understand their needs and concerns, as well as actively seeking their feedback so that you can continue to improve your product or service.
- For employees, relationship-building might involve taking the time to get to know your staff on a personal level, showing genuine interest in their lives, understanding their motivations, and recognizing their unique efforts.

If you want to get the most out of the people you're leading, they need to know you're on their side. They need to know that you care about them as human beings, not just as worker bees in a grand hive. Everyone is unique, and there are times when we struggle to connect with a colleague. Clashes between employees and upper management occur regularly. Leading effectively requires you to see beyond petty personal differences and seek out the common ground that will enable all parties to share in the bounty of success.

Trait 3: Decisiveness

There's nothing worse than a leader that won't lead. A good leader knows that she must sometimes make a difficult decision with limited information. And that the repercussions of her decision will affect not only the course of the organization but also the lives of the individuals who work there. These high-stakes choices can be daunting, but a wise leader understands that decisiveness is crucial to maintaining momentum and progress. Having a bias toward *action* ensures that the organization keeps moving, even if the best path forward is not obvious. The mere act of traversing along at least one path is almost always better than halting your procession entirely.

New leaders tend to fear the cost of making a *bad choice* more than the cost of making *no choice at all*. It is natural to have such an instinctual response. But it is essential to understand that failure is common along the path of success; some of the most valuable insights and innovations ever discovered have been derived via failure and serendipity. Indecision, on the other hand, can lead to stagnation, missed opportunities, and a lack of trust from your team. Hence, it is paramount that leaders embrace *decisiveness*— making informed choices swiftly and confidently, even when the situation is riddled with complexity and the best course of action cannot be readily known.

Trait 4: Authenticity
Authenticity in leadership is a multifaceted concept, rooted in the premise that leaders should be:

- True to their character,
- Transparent with their intentions,
- And consistent in their actions.

Employees of the modern workplace are no longer content to follow "the boss" solely because of her designated role. Instead, they seek out leaders who inspire. Leaders who exhibit genuineness, who are relatable, and who demonstrate empathy. As a result, authenticity in leadership has become increasingly important in cultivating a motivated and dedicated workforce.

To be "authentic" is to be *vulnerable*. The closer you work with your team, the more cognizant they will be of both your successes and your failures. So don't try to mask either one. Authentic leaders don't hide behind a mask of invulnerability or perfection, but rather, they showcase their humanity. They aren't afraid to admit that they don't have all the answers because they understand that vulnerability breeds trust and respect. And they know that their transparency can inspire a team to strive for *growth* rather than perfection.

Trait 5: A Strong Work Ethic

One of the most prevalent traits shared among the titans of industry is their unwavering work ethic. A strong work ethic is crucial in leadership. Long work hours not only correlate with your personal daily output, they also serve to set the bar for the level of commitment and diligence that each team member might be expected to attain. Leaders who work tirelessly not only earn the respect and trust of the team, but also inspire them to press on and keep their nose to the grindstone, even during those moments when all they want to do is quit. Demonstrating a commitment to hard work implies a dedication to the organization and its mission.

Trait 6: Consistency

Nobody wants to work with Dr. Jekyll and Mr. Hyde. Duplicity breeds uncertainty, doubt, and fear. Such emotions are not the sort we aim to manifest in our quest to build a reliable, stable, and productive workforce. When a leader's behaviors and expectations fluctuate, her wavering disposition can give way to confusion and insecurity among the staff. In contrast, *consistency* in leadership paves the way for a stronger and more cohesive team dynamic. This entails showing up at the office on time each morning, with a high degree of enthusiasm, energy, and a steadfast commitment to the company mission. Of course, it's easy to remain consistent when everything on your ship is in order and things are progressing swimmingly. But truly great leaders have the ability to maintain their composure even when the seas get rough and there are turbulent waters ahead.

Trait 7: Agility

Great leaders are agile. The capricious nature of the business climate calls upon us to adapt to market changes, shifting strategies, and emergent technologies, all while remaining focused on our overarching vision. Great leaders understand that, though there is immense value in *focus*, the stubborn adherence to a single path can cause innovation to stall. Remaining blinkered in our endeavors can inhibit growth and impede our ability to spot potentially fruitful opportunities lurking on the hazy horizon. Agility, in this context, doesn't suggest *impulsivity* or a lack of strategy, but rather a calculated *flexibility* that enables us to pivot accordingly should the territory of the business world change.

Trait 8: Resilience

Resilience refers to the ability to skillfully respond to and recover from adversity. This is not to say that we are impervious to failure or immune to disappointment. On the contrary, a resilient leader understands that failure is common. Most business ventures fail. There is no mathematical formula for success. (If one existed, then all mathematicians would be billionaires.) Instead, good leaders know that the key to long-term success lies in their ability to bounce back from failure quickly—to learn from the experience and keep moving forward, despite the white noise of criticism that might emanate from external observers or internal doubts.

Resilient leaders don't dwell on their mistakes; they acknowledge and grow from them. They use these lessons to improve upon their strategy and make course corrections when appropriate. This trait is essential because it not only affords the leader with the emotional wherewithal to navigate through tough times, but it also incites the entire team to ride out the storm.

Resilience is contagious.

The reason that Sylvester Stallone's "Rocky" franchise has made over $1.5 billion in box office sales is not because Rocky wins every fight. Instead, our admiration for the character stems from our realization that Rocky never quits. He gets knocked down, and he gets right back up again, in every single movie. If a leader is able to manifest a similar level of determination and resolve, then she too can serve as an inspirational figurehead for her team— inspiring them to meet challenges head-on and persist when times get tough.

Ch. 2: Develop your personal leadership style

Do you need to be a tyrant to lead?

When people imagine what a leader with a commanding presence might look like, they tend to envision a person with a classic *Type A personality*. The term has managed to permeate popular culture since it was first described by the American cardiologists Meyer Friedman and Ray Rosenman in 1974. In their book *Type A Behavior and Your Heart*, Friedman and Rosenman described a typical "hot head." We all know the type. The boss who barks orders at employees, screams profanities, and works feverishly atop his desk—as if he were competing with the devil themself. Friedman and Rosenman listed several traits to describe such a persona. They are:

- aggressive
- anxious
- exacting
- hyperalert
- impatient
- impulsive
- pugnacious
- status-conscious
- time conscious

- extremely competitive

Such achievement-motivated people tend to live life at a faster pace. They may become impatient and aggressive when others can't keep up with their demands. Type A personalities also love to work. And they have trouble comprehending why other people do not wish to commit the same amount of time to the chore of empire-building.

The preceding list of attributes comprises the default set of traits that many new entrepreneurs assume a boss in a leadership role should project. But in the modern workplace, such characteristics do not necessarily correlate with leadership success. Instead, the management of a 21st-century labor force often calls upon the boss to exhibit a wider range of abilities.

Like me, you've probably had the opportunity to work for several managers during your lifetime. And you've probably noticed that none of them had the same leadership style. My first boss took a hands-on approach to job training, taking the time to show each employee exactly how he wanted each task done. When we made a mistake, he would take us aside and talk to us about what had happened. He would ask us questions to make sure each staff member understood the situation, and then we would discuss how the problem could be fixed. In essence, this boss was a *facilitator*, guiding the employees through those early life lessons.

I've also experienced a very different leadership style in one of my later corporate jobs. Most people would have surely diagnosed this second boss as having a Type A personality.

- She was an incredibly hard-working woman with a schedule so full that (to this day) I still can't believe she managed to complete so many daily objectives.
- She didn't have time for long conversations or encouraging pep talks.
- She told us what we needed to do in the fewest possible words, allotted one minute for questions, and then left us to sink or swim.
- She pushed us to excel at our jobs, inciting us to mirror the way *she* worked, urging us to try to achieve the standard *she* set.

Even though I knew I didn't want to lead the same way she did, I appreciated the way she pushed me to develop and grow. I learned to work hard—to roll up my sleeves and grind for hours to make a deadline. I also learned to communicate my ideas quickly and clearly, a skill I have used to my advantage throughout my career.

In recounting the preceding stories, my aim is to contrast the leadership styles of these two bosses. I noted the disparity in their styles of communication, their approach to task management, and the manner by which they directed their staff. Later in life, when considering the type of persona that I should manifest when communicating with my own staff, I was quick to realize the importance of remaining agile in my approach.

In Daniel Goleman's 2001 book *Primal Leadership*, he described six styles of leadership that his research team observed in the contemporary workplace. He labeled them:

1. Commanding
2. Pacesetting
3. Democratic
4. Affiliative
5. Coaching
6. Visionary

Let's take a more in-depth look at each style now.

Goleman's 6 Leadership Styles

Leadership Style 1: Commanding

Most of us have had exposure to a boss or leader who invoked the "commanding" leadership style. I.e., someone who donned a persona reminiscent of a military general. Those who utilize this style don't tolerate employee questions or delayed compliance. They need to have complete control over their environment and their workers at all times, and they will not accept any challenge to the contrary. Such bosses adopt an *"If I say it, you do it"* approach to leadership. While brash, Goleman was quick to note that this management style does have its place. In emergency situations—such as those experienced in combat—there's simply no time to challenge the decisions of the leader. In fact, doing so could be deadly. The inability of the team to execute commands swiftly could result in catastrophic outcomes or even lost lives.

Thankfully, in the modern office, most of us are not leading our teams through such dire circumstances. However, almost all companies will eventually experience a crisis of some sort—such as a looming bankruptcy, an inability to make payroll, or a labor revolt. The *commanding* leadership style may be appropriate in such crises. But it is usually not considered to be a viable approach for long-term ventures. And during the typical course of business, this leadership style should be used sparingly. For obvious reasons, working under the looming shadow of a commanding tyrant can result in decreased employee morale and job dissatisfaction.

Leadership Style 2: Pacesetting

The pacesetting leadership style emphasizes the importance of meeting deadlines and surpassing targets established by the boss (aka the "pacesetter"). The boss's personal skillset is the benchmark by which all employees must gauge their efforts. The pacesetting leadership style is commonly assumed by the founders of new companies. This is expected given that the founder's outlier skill with her craft is likely to be the very reason that prompted her to start her own company in the first place. So, it's natural for her to expect everyone else under her management to match her own work pace and skill level.

Of course, one of the obvious problems that results from this management style is that not all new hires will be able to keep up with the boss. Expecting everyone to perform at this level can lead to employee burnout, lowered morale, and a high turnover rate. Additionally, the pacesetting style often leaves little room for creativity or innovation, as the focus is primarily on meeting set benchmarks and not on less quantifiable (but possibly more fortuitous) workplace endeavors.

Therefore, while the pacesetting style can be effective in the short-term or during crunch times when deadlines need to be met, it is often not sustainable in the long term. Leaders should be aware of the potential downsides and consider incorporating elements from other leadership styles to create a more balanced work environment.

Leadership Style 3: Democratic

The democratic style is all about the *will of the majority*. Leaders who embrace the democratic approach strive to hear the opinion of each employee at the table. They then arrive at a business decision based on consensus. This stance helps to develop a strong sense of comradery among the staff, and it has the benefit of making the employees feel valued for more than just the tasks they manage. Team members come to believe that "their voice counts," and hence they are less likely to object to company decisions.

However, as anyone who has ever watched C-SPAN knows, the wheels of democracy turn very slowly. A democratic committee often involves a lot of discussion and negotiation, which can lead to delays in decision-making. This can be problematic in situations where swift action is needed. Moreover, while having everyone's input can lead to more informed decisions and greater buy-in from the staff, it's not always the case that the majority opinion equates to the best course of action. The business world often calls upon the boss to make lightning-fast judgments with minimal data. During such moments, there is simply not enough time to poll the entire staff for their opinion on each matter. By the time all the relevant people have been gathered, and the crew has managed to come to an agreement, the window of opportunity may have already closed, and the consensus may no longer be viable.

Leadership Style 4: Affiliative

The affiliative leadership style focuses on building positive work relationships. Affiliative bosses are forever striving to maintain harmony among the staff. Their oft-cited primary objective is to "put people first." They may be less focused on achieving corporate goals and more focused on the needs of each employee. Such a parental role has both positive and negative consequences. On the positive, deep trusting relationships can develop between the boss and the employees, resulting in a workplace in which each team member is intent on looking out for the well-being of the group. On the negative side, the boss's attempt to look after the personal needs of each staff member may inhibit her from providing constructive feedback, which is essential if each employee is to push beyond their current boundaries in pursuit of ever loftier goals.

Affiliative bosses must understand that, though we all want to create a wonderful workspace for our employees, we also want to pursue increasingly demanding business objectives. We have a responsibility to the people we lead, not just to encourage them, but also to let them know when they've underperformed. When we do this, we give them a chance to learn and grow, which is crucial if we want the same for our company.

Leadership Style 5: Coaching

The coaching leadership style is focused on discovering the unique abilities of each individual employee and the development of a plan to address any current deficiencies. Like a football coach trying to get the most value out of each player, bosses who employ the *coaching style* will work with each employee to realize the individual's true potential. The ideal result is the eventual betterment of all parties involved—the employee, the team, and the company. Such an approach can have profound, positive effects on employee morale, as each member of the team is given a chance to improve and become their best self. Employees are empowered in their roles and receive regular feedback on their performance. However, this approach requires a significant time investment from the boss. Thus, this style may be ill-suited for larger companies where the manager-to-employee ratio is limited.

It's also worth noting that not all employees respond well to a coaching style. Some individuals resist interpersonal feedback of this sort and would prefer a more hands-off approach. Additionally, it's not uncommon for there to be a disparity between a boss's intention to help an employee excel, and the employee's perception of the boss's input. Not all advice is welcomed. If not handled correctly, the coaching strategy can devolve into mere micromanagement.

Leadership Style 6: Visionary

Sometimes, the best way to motivate your staff to do their best work is to inspire them with a vision of a noble goal or a brighter tomorrow. This sentiment is so common in the tech world that it is often the subject of comical ridicule. Fans of Mike Judge's TV series "Silicon Valley" might be familiar with a running joke on the show. Each tech company in Silicon Valley insists that they are about to "change the world," no matter how trite or inconsequential their little mobile app might be.

While the notion is sometimes silly, at least their heart is in the right place. If a company is led by a visionary leader who genuinely believes in the mission and who really thinks that her product or service has legitimate existential value to humankind, then her enthusiasm for her mission may be contagious. And it may inspire her team to work towards achieving her vision with increased dedication and passion. This sentiment can help create a positive work culture wherein everyone is motivated to contribute their best efforts toward the success of the company's objectives.

The visionary leader focuses her efforts on getting her people to understand where they would like the company to go. Then, she sets them free to use their own skills to find the best way to contribute to the team effort. When applied correctly, the visionary style can be quite effective. Of all the six leadership styles identified by Daniel Goleman, his research team concluded that workers had the highest job satisfaction when they were led by a visionary.

Let's Review

Each of the preceding six leadership styles has its strengths and weaknesses. Deciding which style to apply is dependent upon the current workplace circumstances in your office. A great leader understands that she must be flexible in her approach to attacking the problems of the day. Just as we all use different styles of discourse with different family members, so too must the boss remain agile enough in her communication style to apply the correct amount of force at the correct time. To drive this point home, let's briefly review each of Goleman's six styles now:

Style 1: Commanding. These leaders like to say, *"To complete this job, just do what I tell you."* A commanding style is best used in situations where the stakes are high and time is limited. If the boss has built up enough relationship equity with her team (i.e., if they trust that she can only afford to make curt responses during a crisis situation), then the commanding style can help get the team through a tough spot.

Style 2: Pacesetting. These leaders like to say, *"To complete this job, do as I do. And please don't fall behind."* This leadership style is often employed by a founder in the early days of a startup. During these times, the boss might indeed be the most capable person on the job. So it makes sense for her to show workers how to do each task, and then to use her own output level as the baseline by which the employees are judged. However, these expectations must be tempered as the company evolves.

Style 3: Democratic. These leaders like to say, *"In your opinion, what is the best way to do this job?"* This approach can be effective when the team members are congenial and the path forward is clear. By tapping into the thoughts and opinions of each employee, we might arrive at solutions that reflect the consensus of the group. But be warned that all groups fracture eventually. Gridlock is common in all democracies. Hence, the democratic style may not always be the most efficient means by which to guide your company through the rigors of competing in a fast-paced market.

Style 4: Affiliative. Leaders using an affiliative style like to say, *"How can we get everyone involved in the completion of this job?"* This style can be particularly effective if the task at hand requires a lot of close collaboration between team members. By fostering a sense of *belonging* amongst the staff, affiliative leaders can enhance team dynamics and coax the employees into working together as a single productive unit.

Style 5: Coaching. Leaders using the coaching style like to say, *"Here is the goal I'd like you to achieve today. Let's see how you do, and then we'll review your results together."* This style can be useful in small teams where the boss has the time to take on the role of a mentor—guiding each employee and encouraging them to expand upon their current skillset gradually.

Style 6: Visionary. These leaders like to say, "*Follow me. If we work hard together, we can accomplish something great.*" People like to follow charismatic leaders. Visionary leaders instill a sense of *purpose* in their team that transcends the banality of mere day-to-day operations. By placing an emphasis on long-term and lofty goals, such leaders are able to focus their teams' efforts on innovative achievements that might someday lead to a bountiful reward. However, while this approach can be incredibly motivating, be warned that history is replete with tales of charismatic leaders who let the majesty of their vision blind them from the cost that was to be paid in its pursuit. Consider the downfall of business titans like Elizabeth Holmes, Adam Neumann, John DeLorean, or Bernie Madoff. Each of these leaders had a grand vision and a charismatic persona that drew others into their orbit. They aroused their investors with promises of revolutionary technology and bountiful returns. However, their single-minded focus on their vision, combined with a lack of transparency and ethical oversights, ultimately led to their demise. Their cases remind us of the importance of balancing one's visionary leadership with grounded realism and ethical integrity. They illustrate the need for leaders to remain receptive to feedback and critique, and to address problems honestly and promptly instead of forever remaining blinkered in their pursuit of a lofty ideal.

Which leadership style is right for you?

It's not easy to determine which of these six leadership styles is appropriate for your current situation. Tuning your workplace interactions requires years of practice and is privy to the disposition of the team members under your employ. Each time you interact with your team in an official capacity, take a moment to consider each of Goleman's six leadership styles, and ask yourself which style you're currently manifesting. Consider if you have selected the correct leadership style given the problem of the day. Of course, we can never know for sure if the management methodology we elect to apply to any given scenario is optimal. However, if you notice that the gears of your company are spinning along like a well-oiled machine (i.e. if your team is working harmoniously toward the completion of your business objectives), then this is a good indication that you have selected your leadership style correctly.

Maintain a List of Practical Daily Habits

We took pains in the previous section to emphasize the importance of *agility* in the leadership game. Good leaders know how to "play jazz." They know how to improvise and adapt to new situations and new obstacles as they reveal themselves along the path of success. However, good leaders also understand the value of *consistency* and *habit*. As the American historian Will Durant once wrote:

We are what we repeatedly do. Excellence, then, is not an act, but a habit.

Meaning that, impressive victories are not the result of hitting a single homerun. Instead, they are the result of the accumulated years of practice that were required to condition an amateur into a professional baseball player. This conditioning only happens by way of habitual practice. If we hope to be an effective leader, we must adopt a similar level of commitment to the daily grind. Habits are the cornerstone of long-term success. The tiny (almost insignificant) actions we take every day accumulate over time and shape who we are and who we will become. Discovering the exact set of habits that you choose to execute each morning is a personal endeavor that should reflect your current stage in business. However, in the following passages, I've listed a few universal workplace habits that should help to inspire the creation of your daily schedule.

Habit 1: Plan tomorrow today

Good leaders don't start their day without a plan. Each morning after you open your eyes and achieve consciousness, a stopwatch is set in your brain. This stopwatch will traverse 16 hours of time. And then, once these 16 hours are complete, you're going to lose consciousness again (i.e., you will fall asleep). In each 24-hour workday, we only have 16 hours to get something done. However, as we all know, most of these 16 hours will not be put to very good use. Life's innumerable chores will forever be eating away at your productivity goals.

- How long does it take you to get dressed?
- How long does it take you to eat breakfast?
- How long does it take you to drive your kids to school?
- How long is your commute to work?
- How long is your lunch break?

- How many hours can you work without getting tired?

The morning rush consumes much of our time. Watercooler chitchat consumes even more. YouTube, Facebook, and Instagram eat up the rest. The mental fatigue that sets in at around six o'clock each evening usually prevents us from doing much more than heating a microwave dinner and watching Netflix before nodding off. While many people insist that they work approximately eight to twelve hours per day, their actual number of productive hours is usually closer to four. Each day presents us with a very narrow window in which we can be productive. By taking a moment (today) to plan out the action steps that must be accomplished tomorrow, we help to ensure that these tasks will actually get done.

Habit 2: Be the most organized person in the room

You're the boss. Which means that you're responsible for ensuring that your team operates with competence, direction, and efficiency. If you show up late at the office and find yourself shuffling through a briefcase full of disorganized papers, this sends a signal to your team that "disorder is acceptable in this office." Obviously, this is not the message we wish to send.

As a leader, your actions set the tone for the workplace. Make it a habit to organize your thoughts, your tasks, your time, your schedule, and your desk. Set a positive example for your team, and this will inspire them to mirror your professionalism.

Habit 3: Keep three sets of goals

On my laptop computer, I have three documents: one labeled "short-term goals," one labeled "medium-term goals," and one labeled "long-term goals." The titles of these documents reveal their contents:

- The "short-term goals" file is for tasks that must be done today. This file functions like my to-do list.
- The "medium-term goals" file describes goals that must be accomplished in the months ahead.
- And my "long-term goals" file functions more like my mission statement or vision board. It contains a list of yearly business objectives as well as a list of things I'd like to accomplish in my life. It functions as my North Star—guiding me toward my ideal destination and helping me to ensure that each of my smaller decisions aligns with my core objectives.

Of course, these files are *living documents*. They change and evolve as I accomplish new tasks, as priorities shift, and as my vision for the future metamorphosizes with each passing year. This is why it's good to save versions of these documents. I don't merely overwrite them when it's time to make an edit. Instead, once a year, I print them out and store the paper copies in an old filing cabinet. Occasionally, I return to these pages and read through them. In glancing at my ancient archive, I often sit in a state of wonder and bemusement—thinking about how much things have changed, how much my business has changed, and how much I have changed. I often mumble to myself, "What was I thinking when I wrote down this goal?" By maintaining such an archive, the files not only serve as a roadmap but also as a reflection of one's personal progress and a testimony to personal growth.

As is the case with so many other business methodologies, we must adopt a strategy of brinkmanship when deciding which goals to attend to. If we concentrate our vision on our lofty long-term goals, then we risk neglecting the immediate task at hand. But if we focus only on each daily vicissitude, then we may lose sight of our long-term objectives, and we might even forget the reason why we took on the leadership role to begin with. Striking the right balance between these two outlooks is critical to maintaining our forward momentum while also driving us toward the fulfillment of our ultimate lifegoals.

Habit 4: Acknowledge the efforts of each team member

An important aspect of being a good leader is keeping people motivated and producing quality work. One of the best ways to do this is to acknowledge individuals when we see the kind of behavior that we value. There are few things employees love more than being recognized for their efforts. By acknowledging those around us for the things they excel at, we encourage them to repeat that specific behavior again. We also increase their general mood and morale. Both effects serve to draw the best work out of our employees. Additionally, recognizing team members promotes a positive workplace culture. It shows that their efforts are not taken for granted, and that every individual's contribution is essential for the company's success.

Habit 5: Work hard, up until the point at which it's time to rest

Recall the previous section in which we noted that each day is comprised of sixteen hours of consciousness followed by eight hours of sleep. Many entrepreneurs are quick to recount an episode of their business career during which they "burned the midnight oil" for several months—all in an effort to complete a project or launch a new product line. Such stories are inspirational and motivational. But the many limitations of the human body often stand in contrast to these harrowing tales. Sustainable success is not achieved via a prolonged disregard for rest and self-care—that's the path to burnout and an early grave. Instead, achieving a healthy work-life balance is essential if we are to promote the sustained levels of creativity and productivity that we'll need to accomplish our business objectives. We'll be discussing this more in Chapter 8. For now, just know that the race to success is a marathon, not a sprint. Most impressive human endeavors are only achieved following a steady and continuous investment of time, effort, and energy.

We don't study productivity and build habits because we aim to devote a minimum amount of time to our labor. Instead, we build good habits because we appreciate how very short our time on this planet is. This is why remaining cognizant of your limited number of daily productive hours is so vital. The brain operates much like any other muscle in the body. As the hands of the clock approach 5, 6, or 7 pm, our brain's ability to keep working diminishes. Just as every good machinist knows the limitations of each tool in his machine shop, so too must we familiarize ourselves with the cognitive limitations of the mind.

Which leadership style are you?

As mentioned before the Introduction, I've prepared a free worksheet for this book. Inside, you'll find a brief quiz which attempts to analyze your disposition and reveal your personal leadership style. If you're reading this book on a Kindle or an iPad, you can click the link below. Or, paperback readers can type the link into your PC or iPhone. Thanks everyone! – Serena

www.tiny.cc/bossleader

Ch. 3: Identify your company's Core Competencies and goals

What are Core Competencies?

In contemporary business literature, the precise definition of the term "core competency" is contested. The original interpretation was authored by the business theorist C.K. Prahalad and the management consultant Gary Hame in their 1990 article for the *Harvard Business Review* entitled "The Core Competence of the Corporation." Here, Prahalad and Hame argued that a company would be best advised to focus its efforts on its most foundational strengths—aka its "core competencies." To determine what the strengths of a company were, they provided a set of formal criteria.

- **Criterion 1**: The product should be in demand from a large variety of markets. For example, if you produce LCD screens, then your product has the potential to be used in millions of devices ranging from computer peripherals to dishwashers and calculators.
- **Criterion 2**: The product should make a significant contribution to the value of the final product. Meaning that the widget you manufacture should be so essential to the creation of the *end-user product* that the producer would find it difficult to complete their manufacturing process without you.

- **Criterion 3**: The product or service should be difficult to imitate. I.e., if one of your competitors ever attempts to replicate your success, then you'd prefer them to have a long road to haul.

Since Prahalad and Hame published their original paper in 1990, the *core competency* concept has become quite popular. Some are quick to note the difference between a "core competency" and a mere "business capability." A *business capability* is just something your business is good at. But technically, a true *core competency* must fulfill each of Prahalad and Hame's three criteria. However, in popular business books, the two concepts are often conflated. We're not going to make a big fuss about the issue here. And since this book is mostly aimed at entrepreneurs starting new businesses or managing new teams, we'll be adopting the looser usage of the term in this chapter. A core competency can be any operation your business performs that is a cut above the same operation performed by your competitors. Let's discuss how you might go about identifying such capabilities.

How to identify your Core Competencies

Tip 1: Brainstorm

The first step in identifying your company's core competencies lies in simply brainstorming over the question, "What are we good at?" There's probably something that your company is known for doing well. This might be any one of a number of capabilities including:

- best customer service
- best aesthetic design
- best quality product

- fastest delivery time
- fastest production time
- highest degree of customizability
- or lowest cost

In examining the preceding list, it's likely that you can identify at least one trait that your company has the potential to excel at. Whether you label these attributes as "core competencies" or simply "business capabilities" is not relevant to our discussion. Rather, our initial objective is to identify and highlight your greatest strengths and the utility of concentrating your focus on the small set of unique skills that will give you a competitive edge in the market.

Tip 2: Critically examine every part of your production process

Another way to reveal your company's strengths and weaknesses is to take a close look at the many processes that are essential to securing the timely delivery of your product or service. Even the humblest small business is reliant upon a multitude of independent processes to function effectively. These might include:

- A distribution or delivery system
- A manufacturing or production process
- A way to procure raw materials or component parts
- Sales and marketing campaigns
- Inventory management and warehousing
- Customer service
- Tech support
- Accounting and financial management

By conducting a detailed examination of the areas of your business that you might have overlooked in the past, you might discover some opportunities for improvement. Such business operations might have the potential to become *core competencies* if they are provided with additional attention and resources.

- For example, you might find that some members of your marketing team have been consistently executing successful campaigns. But they lack the advanced tools or technology needed to fully capitalize on future ventures. Further investment might amplify their efforts.
- Or, you might discover that your product design process produces beautiful creations but is not well streamlined, and the technique has not been formalized. Taking the time to refine this process could enable your team to launch new products more quickly, hence turning the procedure into a core competency.

By taking the time to examine each node in your supply chain—from the most high-profile tasks to the most mundane—you have the potential to uncover hidden strengths and areas for improvement. Nurturing these business functions might enable you to reveal the competitive edge you'll need to drive future business growth.

Tip 3: Review your mission statement, company values, or goals

When attempting to identify your core competencies, it might be best to start with your company's *mission statement*. If you're currently employed in a large company, the mission statement might be hanging on a plaque in a forgotten corner of your reception area. Or if you've just started a new company, perhaps you haven't even gotten around to making one yet.

The company mission statement is the first mechanism by which we broadcast our goals to the outside world. A mission statement is a single sentence that describes why an organization exists and what its *modus operandi* is. It often hints at the product or service that the company produces and attempts to describe the values of the founders to the potential customer. Let's examine the mission statement of three well-known tech brands.

- **PayPal**: "To build the web's most convenient, secure, and cost-effective payment solution."
- **Google**: "To organize the world's information and make it universally accessible and useful."
- **LinkedIn**: "To connect the world's professionals to make them more productive and successful."

When identifying the set of business operations that you aim to focus on, it can be beneficial to gauge the degree to which your actions coincide with the goals espoused by your company's mission statement. If the core competencies you've selected do not seem to be conducive to fulfilling these objectives, then perhaps you should rethink your list. However, it is also the case that long-running businesses stray from their initial mission quite often.

- **Virgin Group** sprung out of Richard Branson's record shop.
- **3M** started as a small mining company in Minnesota.
- **Amazon** was originally a small online bookstore. CEO Jeff Bezos used to deliver the book packages to the post office himself each morning.

Business goals and scope change over time, just like people do. As a leader, we must accept that such changes are inevitable, all while striving to focus our efforts on the business operations that are most likely to bring about the fulfillment of our stated mission.

Tip 4: Research your competitors

Given that a *core competency* refers to some aspect of business that your company excels at beyond your competitor's faculties, developing an understanding of your competitors' strengths and weaknesses is useful when identifying areas for growth. Indeed, your core competencies might not even be apparent to you until you view your company through your competitor's lens. Use whatever means you have at your disposal to gather information about their operations. Ask yourself questions such as:

- How well is their main product line selling?
- What is their pricing strategy?
- How do they market themselves?
- What technology do they utilize to be more productive?
- What partnerships are most advantageous to them?
- What customer segments do they target?

Maybe one competitor has a well-known brand, while another offers excellent customer service. Perhaps one struggles with timely delivery, while another lacks a strong online presence. Try to be as objective as possible in your analysis. Remember, our goal is not to merely perform an academic critique of our competitors' shortcomings. Instead, we aim to identify potential opportunities for market differentiation. And then, to alter our own business operations to capitalize upon these discoveries.

Tip 5: Have open discussions with both your customers and your staff

As we move up the corporate ladder, it can become increasingly difficult to keep track of each product that exits our front doors. This can be a particularly pressing problem in large companies where the senior leadership might not be directly involved in day-to-day operations. Their seat at the top of the castle might prevent them from noticing the fine cracks forming along the foundation. To overcome this myopia, it's beneficial to periodically conduct interviews with both your customers and staff. By making an effort to hold such open discussions, we might obtain insights that engender a more nuanced understanding of the company's core competencies.

Here are some key points you might want to consider for such exchanges:

- **Ensure anonymity**: When people feel that their responses will not be held against them, they are more likely to provide honest and valuable feedback.
- **Ask open-ended questions**: Encourage participants to share their thoughts *freely* rather than simply answer with a "yes" or "no" response.
- **Engage multiple perspectives**: Don't just focus on your top-performing employees or your most vocal customers. Different perspectives can lead to a more comprehensive understanding of your product or service.
- **Don't use web forms**: Nobody likes to fill out forms on the internet. And the subset of respondents who do take the time to fill out such forms may not be representative of your customer base. Try to conduct real conversations when possible.

- **Look for patterns in each response**: If multiple employees or customers independently cite the same strengths or weakness, then this is an area of your business that you should consider attending to.
- **Act on the feedback**: Don't let each valuable insight go to waste. Implement changes based on the responses and set up a venue by which you can reinitiate the conversation and follow up with the respondent if possible.

How to conduct a SWOT Analysis

To best reveal your company's core competencies, it's helpful to conduct a quarterly SWOT analysis. A SWOT analysis is a strategic planning method that attempts to aid the business owner or team leader in evaluating her company's viability by assessing it's:

- Strengths
- Weaknesses
- Opportunities
- Threats

If you've never attempted such an analysis, it's probably best to keep things simple. Pull out a piece of paper and draw four columns. Then, in each column, make a list that reflects each of the preceding four factors. We'll describe each factor now.

Factor 1: List your Strengths

In a SWOT analysis, *strengths* are defined as "all the internal positive attributes and resources that give a company a competitive advantage." Hence, your first step is to list the unique strengths that set your company apart from the competition. These attributes can include your core competencies, as discussed in the previous section. But may also comprise less quantifiable properties like your company's reputation, service record, or existing business relationships.

Factor 2: List your Weaknesses

In a SWOT analysis, *weaknesses* are defined as "all the areas in a company that need improvement and are potentially hindering its development." No company is without its flaws. Your ability to recognize the areas in which your organization is faltering is crucial for business growth. Some typical company weaknesses might include outdated technology, limited financial resources, subpar customer service, or slow delivery times.

Factor 3: List your Opportunities

In a SWOT analysis, *opportunities* are defined as "any emergent factor or trend that a company might capitalize upon to achieve market growth." These might include any upcoming development that could potentially increase demand for your product or make your product more saleable in some other fashion. Identifying such opportunities early allows the business owner to strategically position her company to stay ahead of the curve.

Factor 4: List your Threats

In a SWOT analysis, *threats* are defined as "all the external factors or challenges that could potentially negatively impact a company's performance or long-term stability." These might include unfavorable economic changes, rising competition, market saturation, or evolving consumer preferences. By identifying these potential hazards, business owners can adapt to shifting market demands, thus ensuring that the company is better prepared to face such challenges should they arise.

Develop a plan of action

Once you've completed your SWOT analysis, take some time to ruminate over it. Hang the paper bearing your four lists (of strengths, weaknesses, opportunities, or threats) on a wall near your desk and glance at it each morning when you enter the office. Give your mind a couple days to acclimate to the data. Then, retrieve the list from the wall and sketch out an action plan for the next quarter. Try to devise a strategy that addresses all four SWOT factors. Such a plan might entail:

- Accelerating or postponing a product launch.
- Ensuring that you have enough cash reserves to compensate for an upcoming lull in the market.
- Gathering customer feedback or testimonials to strengthen your product offering.
- Establishing a procedure to monitor your top competitor's upcoming product release.
- Designing new features that will better differentiate your offer.
- Making efforts to personalize the customer experience or improve your customer service.
- Outsourcing non-essential tasks to free up internal resources.

There are limitless business operations that companies must perform each day to stay competitive and solvent. The SWOT analysis encourages us to objectively evaluate our current market standing and identify the points of friction that are preventing us from accelerating our growth. In short, it helps us to envision "where we want to be." By identifying our strengths, addressing our weaknesses, seizing opportunities, and mitigating threats, we hope to chart a path to long-term success in an ever-changing business landscape.

Setting S.M.A.R.T. Goals

Now that we've identified some areas of your business that you'd like to develop, how shall we go about ensuring that the goals of this enterprise are achieved? As we've all experienced before, merely jotting down your objectives on a to-do list does not ensure their completion. Instead, I suggest setting *SMART goals*.

SMART goals were invented by George T. Doran and originally enumerated in the November 1981 issue of *Management Review*. Here, Doran advised that business goals should have five attributes. They should be:

- **S**pecific
- **M**easurable
- **A**ssignable
- **R**ealistic
- **T**ime-bound

Let's review each one now.

Attribute 1: Specific

Your goal should be clear and well-defined. Vague or generalized goals (i.e., "I want to increase sales and make more money") are not helpful because they don't provide sufficient direction regarding the process by which one might bring about the objective. Hence, when crafting your goals, try to precisely identify what a "success" would look like. For example:

I want to increase the sales of Product X by 15% over the next quarter.

Attribute 2: Measurable

You should ideally be able to objectively measure the degree to which you have attained your goal. If an objective is not measurable, it is almost impossible to determine whether you are making progress toward the goal's successful completion or not. Metrics or milestones should be identified to track the progress of the goal. In our preceding example, we identified "the sales of Product X" as our primary metric. Here, our progress is easy to quantify since collecting the incoming sales figures should be a relatively straightforward procedure. However, when it comes to goals of a more ethereal nature (e.g., "I want my employees to respect me more"), the method by which you would gauge the desired outcome is not clear. Try to avoid statements like this when crafting SMART goals.

Attribute 3: Assignable

We've all had the experience of walking into an office with the intent of retrieving a specific file or progress report, only to leave with our hands empty and a room full of befuddled employees— each looking to each other and asking, "Who was supposed to be in charge of that?"

If you're merely setting SMART goals for your own personal objectives, then you don't need to spend much time fretting over *goal assignability*. All your goals are up to *you* to complete.

However, when working with a team, *assignability* is crucial to ensuring the successful completion of each objective. Goals may be assigned to individual employees or to entire teams, but only *one* person should be tasked with logging and reporting on the team's progress. The act of selecting one (and only one) person to be the *archivist* of the team's pursuits helps to alleviate the common communication problems that arise when multiple people are responsible for different aspects of a complex project. Assigning one person to collect and collate this data ensures that you (the boss) will be able to track the team's progress as they work toward the completion of the objective.

Attribute 4: Realistic

Your goal should be something that you and your team can realistically be expected to attain. For example, setting a goal to "Increase sales by 900% this year" might not be achievable if your current resources and market conditions don't support such a dramatic rise. While it's important to choose objectives that prompt your team to reach ever-increasing heights, setting unachievable goals can result in frustration and burnout. Hence, before setting a goal, consider the resources you have at your disposal, and evaluate all the relevant factors that ensure that the goal is within reach.

Attribute 5: Time-bound

Parkinson's Law states that:

Work expands so as to fill the time available for its completion.

Meaning that, if you give an employee two days to do an assignment, then it will be completed in two days. But if you give an employee two weeks to do the work, then it will take him two weeks to do it. Goals that are not created with a firm deadline in mind are less likely to be accomplished on time. The daily catastrophes of life will forever be striving to pull our focus away from our primary objectives. Setting a hard deadline for a task's completion ensures that the cruciality of the task remains paramount in the mind of the employee. Looming deadlines have a funny way of prodding people to action.

Let's Review

In this chapter, we have introduced three powerful techniques that will amplify your ability to select and accomplish business objectives.

- By identifying your company's *core competencies*, you will be able to focus your efforts on the aspects of your business that are most likely to result in a competitive advantage.
- Conducting a *SWOT Analysis* (of your Strengths, Weaknesses, Opportunities, and Threats) helps to reveal the areas where your business operations could evolve to enable you to seize upon emerging market opportunities.
- And, by setting *SMART Goals* (Specific, Measurable, Assignable, Realistic, and Time-bound) we can ensure that our team has a methodology by which each objective can be effectively managed and pursued.

I hope I was able to convince you of the utility to be garnered when these three concepts are working in unison. When you're able to reveal your company's core competencies via a SWOT analysis, and utilize SMART goals to pursue the identified market opportunities, that's when the magic happens. The plan that results from the application of these methodologies should provide you with a powerful framework on which to construct your business strategy and plot a course to success.

Ch. 4: How to assemble and manage your dream team

People are complicated. We all have our own little idiosyncrasies that make us unique. We possess strengths that make us an asset. And weaknesses that leave us frustrated and vulnerable. When you bring a group of people together, circumstances can become infinitely more complex as each human quirk mixes together into a rich psychological stew. This is why team dynamics can be such an enigma. If you've ever been a part of a dysfunctional team, you may have found it to be one of the most frustrating and stressful experiences of your work life. On the other hand, a productive and convivial team functions like a well-oiled machine—able to make even difficult or unpleasant tasks seem effortless.

I remember being part of a team that was brought together for a project that was expected to take three months to complete. It was an amazing group of people who were each intent on giving it their all. The communication was clear, respectful, and focused. We all got along well and seemed to naturally take to the roles we were expected to fill. It was a wonderful experience, and after only two months, we were finished. We completed the project in record time and disbanded, each member moving on to other things.

Approximately six months later, the team was reformed to tackle another project of a similar sort. I was excited to work with everyone again and had a spring in my step as I approached the office door. But, when I arrived at the meeting room, I discovered that one team member had moved across the country after getting married. They had been replaced by another member of the department who had since taken over her responsibilities. The swap was noteworthy, but I didn't initially give it much thought, and we all got on with the project.

Unfortunately, a repeat of our previous success was not in the cards. The difference in the team dynamic was immediately noticeable. The smooth communication and effective meetings were gone. Everything seemed to drag on for twice as long as it needed to, and everyone seemed on edge whenever we entered the meeting room. In the end, it took us around four months to complete the project, and the results were less than stellar.

After such a debacle, it's tempting to assign the blame to the newest member of the team. However, when I look back at that time now, I can't pinpoint a moment when the new hire did anything wrong. Obviously, the balance of the team was thrown off by the loss of its most unifying member. But the new person wasn't a bad teammate. His work was good. It's just that the comradery of the group was disrupted. When the social norms we had successfully acclimated to in the previous project were agitated, we were unable to return to our former project groove.

- We argued about our roles.
- We disagreed about the best way to complete each task.
- We had difficult communication problems that caused us to miss deadlines.

In retrospect, I now recognize these problems for what they were—the inevitable result of poor team dynamics. Thankfully, as business leaders, we have a couple tools at our disposal to manage such obstacles before they devolve into quagmires. Let's discuss these tools now.

Introducing Tuckman's Ladder

Bruce Tuckman was an American psychologist who was best known for his research on group dynamics. While working at the Naval Medical Research Institute in Maryland, he created a useful taxonomy for organizing the observed behaviors of workers in small groups. In his 1965 paper *Developmental Sequence in Small Groups*, Tuckman introduced his model, which was later termed "Tuckman's Ladder." His system attempts to provide us with a template for organizing the familiar tensions that we all experience whenever a group of complex humans come together to complete a project.

Tuckman breaks down the process of group dynamics into five stages. As team leader, your ability to recognize which stage your team is currently positioned at can be quite valuable. By familiarizing yourself with the concepts depicted in Tuckman's Ladder, you might be better able to modulate your behaviors, angling your efforts to provide the best type of assistance to your team at each rung of their climb. We'll discuss the five parts of Tuckman's Ladder here.

Stage 1: Forming

As the name implies, the "forming stage" is when teams form together. Just as the concrete that is used to form the foundation of your home must first be mixed and allowed to set before it can support the construction of the house, so too must your team be given time to establish their own firm foundation. Team members are usually selected because of a specific skill they bring to the project. The role that each person will play begins to take shape. People infer what is acceptable (in terms of behavior and methods of discourse), and they learn what is expected in terms of performance. If there are problems among the group members, they tend to lie dormant; nobody wants to spoil the mood during the honeymoon period. Hence, it can sometimes be difficult to get an accurate picture of how each team member is feeling at this point in the process.

As a leader, your job is to unite everyone on the team during this stage of the game. This could be accomplished in many ways, such as by organizing team-building exercises or social events that help to foster relationships between employees. Your efforts should also focus on clearly defining the roles and responsibilities of each team member, establishing the project's objectives, and outlining the expectations for job performance. This is also the time when you should establish the methods by which team members will communicate with each other and how decisions will be made when the input of the team is called for.

Stage 2: Storming

The honeymoon is over. This is the stage when people's true feelings and personalities come to light. As employees become more comfortable with each other, they will naturally begin to express their opinions more. If all goes well, trust should be formed between the group members during this stage, and everyone should have a clearer idea of what their role entails. However, no project goes well all the time. Tensions rise as deadlines loom. Inevitably, some conflict will arise. As people get more comfortable sharing their opinions (and more comfortable disagreeing with each other), the undercurrents of tension that may have been present in *Stage 1* come bursting to the surface.

As team leader, it's important to facilitate the resolution of any emerging conflict instead of just trying to suppress it. Suppressed conflict will only lead to more explosive arguments later on. By helping employees reconcile their differences, you'll enable the team to continue functioning properly. Remind the team that you're all working toward a common goal. Remember to practice *active listening* and focus on guiding the team members to a solution that they can mutually benefit from. At the end of the day, professionalism is expected in a work environment, so ensuring an atmosphere of respect will net you the best results.

Stage 3: Norming

In this stage, everyone comes to terms with their role in the team. They accept the other members and begin to truly work together toward accomplishing their assigned goals. There is a sense of common understanding within the group. Once a team has reached this stage, team members start sorting out their conflicts themselves, as they have developed a trust for one another that allows for open communication. Finally, each employee feels comfortable with their role and now has an opportunity to focus on the task at hand. Since most interpersonal issues have been resolved by this point, you are free to help guide each individual team member to fulfill her role to the best of her abilities. When doing this, it's important to provide guidance but also to encourage each member to be self-sufficient—autonomously handling incoming contingencies whenever possible.

Stage 4: Performing

At this point, the team is sailing smoothly. They're talking the talk and walking the walk. To-do list items are getting ticked off rapidly, and success looms on the horizon. There may still be some conflict here and there, but overall the team members have fully realized their roles and are working together professionally and cohesively.

When a team is performing well, it's important to not interfere with the balance. The team is doing exactly what it needs to do, so let them do it. This doesn't mean you should go completely hands-off and stop interacting. The team may still have questions that need answering, need help managing their time, or want your advice on how to handle a project-related issue. Be present and available to the people you're leading. However, allow them to come to you when they need assistance instead of jumping in every time you see something that might be an issue.

Stage 5: Adjourning

This can be the hardest stage because it's where everything comes to an end. When a big project has been completed, it's just a matter of time before everyone goes their separate ways. In this stage, it can be incredibly helpful for team members if you, as the leader, try to bring a sense of closure to the end of a project. This is the time for the group to look back over the process. We'll talk about team evaluations next, but first, it's important to celebrate the success of the team. It's also important to realize that individuals may be returning to previous roles or moving on to other prospects.

Moving up and down Tuckman's Ladder

When utilizing Tuckman's Ladder, we should consider two important notes:

- First, know that teams rarely progress up each rung of Tuckman's Ladder sequentially and without incident. Situations inevitably arise that prompt the group to return back down to the storming stage, where the team will be forced to consider and debate the best way to manage the newfound obstacle, and then to acclimate to the altered project scope. If, during the course of the project, the team encounters yet another unforeseen threat, then they may have to return to the storming stage again. During complex projects, teams might be forced to move up and down Tuckman's Ladder several times before the job is done.

- Second, know that each rung of the Ladder may call upon the boss to utilize a different leadership style. Depending on the disposition of your team, the boss may have to adopt different strategies to effectively navigate the issue of the day. For instance, during the storming stage, the boss may need to be more assertive, providing clear guidance and establishing the norms by which the team discourse is to commence.

As we have attempted to stress throughout this book, good leaders know how to remain agile in their approach. They understand that every team is unique, and they are able to adapt their leadership style to suit the parameters of the project and the individual needs of each employee. By striving to remain cognizant of your team's temperament and their current position on the many rungs of Tuckman's Ladder, the leader can help her team successfully navigate the unique challenges of each stage of the objective more effectively.

Empowering your team with SOPs

Standard Operating Procedures (SOPs) are an essential part of any business. They are the "operations manual" for your company—comprising all documented procedures for individual office functions and company-wide processes. Their purpose is to help employees perform tasks and make decisions in a manner that is consistent with how the boss herself would do them.

My first exposure to the world of SOPs came when I got my first job at my college campus. I worked in the gym, and it was my responsibility to train the new incoming employees. Since each employee was a student like me, our turnover rate was understandably high. And yet, the management at the gym had never bothered to create an SOP. There was no employee training documentation at all. This made my job particularly tedious because, each time a new employee would hop on board, I'd have to verbally describe each task in meticulous detail—again and again and again…

Eventually, I decided to take matters into my own hands and do my boss's job for him. I created the SOPs for my gym and documented our entire onboarding process. It took some time and several revisions, but it eventually made my job much easier. When I graduated college and left my job at the gym, they had built up quite a repository of documented processes—which is still in use to this day.

The Many Types of SOPs

There are many different types of SOPs, and each company uses a slightly different style. But the general goal is to devise a system by which business functions are performed consistently by clearly enumerating the procedures to be performed. Let's take a moment to discuss some SOP terminology. The words *policy*, *process*, and *procedure* are often used interchangeably. But there is a subtle difference between them.

- A **policy** is a company-wide rule that all employees should follow. For example, a "company policy" might outline the safety guidelines that all employees are to adhere to before entering a lab or a construction site.
- A **process** explains the sequence of actions that should be undertaken to achieve a particular outcome. For instance, the "hiring process" might entail many procedures—from posting a job opening to conducting interviews with potential candidates.
- A **procedure** identifies the exact steps that are required to complete a specific task. For example, the procedure for refilling the print cartridge in the office printer might include several steps, such as a description of how to remove the spent cartridge and how to insert a new one.

Not all company SOPs scrutinize the exact wording to be used when describing the multiple levels of tasks each business performs. And not all company processes can be reduced to a procedural (or algorithmic) format. But it is beneficial to understand the distinction between these concepts so that you can create a set of effective SOPs that suit the unique needs of your company. As the size of your company grows, the complexity of its operations will inevitably increase, resulting in ever more abstract policies.

Additionally, the format and medium you choose to create your SOPs will also vary. We'll list four SOP types here:

- **Simple SOPs** function just like a to-do list does. They contain a step-by-step set of instructions that are needed to complete a certain office procedure. For young companies, Simple SOPs are the only SOPs you'll need.
- **Hierarchical SOPs** are for larger companies. They attempt to organize all business processes and procedures based on the level of complexity or the positioning of the task in the organizational hierarchy.
- **Flowcharts** are sometimes used when the employee needs to follow a procedure in which multiple events might happen. For example, a customer service representative might use a flowchart to determine the best course of action when dealing with a customer complaint on the phone. A visual representation of the procedure can help the employee make quick and effective decisions during the interaction.
- **Multimedia SOPs** are the preferred type in my office. Since most of our activities take place digitally, our SOPs are written in Microsoft Word documents and feature embedded images and video. The videos primarily consist of screen recordings, showing employees how to perform a certain operation in one of our many software apps. By combining the text, imagery, and video into one document, we've found this arrangement to be the best way to describe a task to a new hire.

Now that you have some idea about the many types of SOPs that are possible, it's time to start creating some SOPs of your own. Here are some tips for getting the process started.

How to write an SOP
Step 1: Decide what you'll be documenting
If the idea of writing your own business operations manual seems like a daunting task, then just take things slow. Don't try to solve each one of your company's problems with one document. Instead, try to enumerate one simple task that you've had to teach people in your office repeatedly—like the procedure for changing the ink in the office printer.

Step 2: Identify your target audience
The level of detail your SOPs require will largely depend on your audience. Are you writing an SOP for a coworker who is already familiar with the company's practices and the technology involved in the task? Or are you writing for a newcomer who has just walked through the door and is currently going through your onboarding process? If you want your SOPs to be effective, then it's crucial to know the type of person who will be reading the SOPs before creating them.

Step 3: Take notes as you do a procedure in your office
Just as none of us know "how" we are able to ride a bicycle, business owners often don't know how they go about completing each of their daily business functions. They've been doing the same task for so long that it has become second nature to them. Hence, the easiest way to start the process of creating your SOPs is to simply take notes as you go about doing the procedure yourself. This might entail typing out each step into a document on your computer. Or, as described above, in my office we often

include pictures, screenshots, or brief videos that help describe the process thoroughly.

Step 4: Take notes as an employee does the procedure

Now that you have a first draft of your instructions completed, it's time to hand them off to an employee and see if they are able to follow your steps. It is during this step in which the gaping holes in your documentation will become apparent. Tasks that are obvious to you may seem all but obvious to your employee. Each question the employee asks is an opportunity for you to fill in the blanks or make changes to the SOPs, all with the intent of presenting a clearer picture of how the task is to be done.

Step 5: Refine and update your SOPs

Remember, you don't have to get everything right on your first attempt. Just as a novel will go through dozens of revisions before being published, so too are you free to revise and revisit your SOPs as the years go by. SOPs should be periodically reviewed and updated as needed. Preferably, individual employees should be allowed and encouraged to modify the documents at will. In this sense, SOPs are *living documents*. Their contents should change, grow, and evolve just as your business does. Ideally, the procedures they outline will be performed with greater efficiency with each passing year.

Why SOPs are so useful

Whether you're running a large team or an office with just one employee, I hope this chapter has convinced you of the value to be had in utilizing a good set of Standard Operating Procedures. One of the most difficult obstacles that new entrepreneurs must overcome lies in their inability to see their company as a set of interconnected modules and procedures. When you finally do come to view your creation that way, you might be surprised at the boost in productivity that follows.

For a perfect example of how profitable a business can be if it relies on formalized procedures, look no further than your local metro area. Note the familiar thriving businesses you'll find there:

- McDonald's
- Burger King
- Taco Bell
- KFC
- Subway

Obviously, the algorithmic process by which these businesses operate has worked well for them. At publication, there are over 200,000 fast-food franchise locations operating in America. Of course, not every company functions via processes that can be formalized as easily as the art of burger-flipping or pizza-spinning. But, when possible, strive to note the opportunities in your workplace that could benefit from a set of SOPs. You don't need to be a fast-food franchise owner to appreciate the financial benefit that comes from such a systems-oriented approach to thinking. As Michael Gerber wrote in his best-selling book *The E-Myth Revisited*:

The system runs the business. The people run the system. In the Franchise Prototype, the system becomes the solution to the problems that have beset all businesses and all human organizations since time immemorial. The system integrates all the elements required to make a business work. It transforms a business into a machine, or more accurately, because

it is so alive, into an organism, driven by the integrity of its parts, all working in concert toward a realized objective.

Ch. 5: How to communicate confidently and assertively

The Importance of Confidence

When I was fresh out of college, I attended a work-related seminar. From the moment the first speaker walked on stage, she had my full attention. From her posture, self-assured stance, and engaging smile, everything about her screamed *confidence*. As she began to speak, I marveled at how comfortable she seemed when discussing her business pursuits.

- She made jokes but remained professional.
- She altered the volume of her voice, sometimes speaking slowly and sometimes letting each syllable boom across the conference hall.
- She engaged with the audience but never once lost control of the conversation.

I looked around the room and I could see that all in attendance were hanging on to every word she uttered. I desperately tried to note each syllable, not wanting to miss a thing. Her words spoke wisdom, and I wanted to make that wisdom mine.

It was only once I got home and read my notes that I realized something that would forever change the way I viewed interpersonal communication: *I already knew everything the speaker had shared that day.*

I was astounded by this revelation. It took me a while to figure out what had happened. But eventually, I understood that it was not the content of her message but her *confidence* that had drawn me in. I realized that one's ability to portray a confident persona during a speech might be a lot more important than the content of the speech itself.

The undercurrent of every instruction you give to your staff contains ancillary data that flows to the senses of each listener. Your body language, vocal tonality, and facial expressions come packaged together to reflect the level of competency you have with the issue at hand. Your confidence (or your lack of confidence) is conveyed via this unspoken language. The ease with which you project your message influences how your message will be received. Indeed, it's not just *what* you say but *how* you say it that shapes the way your instructions will be accepted. Understanding this crucial aspect of communication can empower you to steer your team with conviction, prompting them to trust in your vision and in your capabilities as a leader.

The Many Styles of Communication

People communicate via many channels. Selecting the correct style of communication to use at any given moment is dependent upon several factors, including the topic of discussion, the relationship of the interlocutors, and the level of emotion being conveyed in the exchange. Understanding the multiple styles by which people converse is crucial for anyone in a leadership role. Let's take a moment to list four communication styles here.

Style 1: Passive

People who use the passive style often communicate the least. They tend to mask their emotions and opinions, thus making it difficult for others to discern what they're thinking. They might also be soft-spoken and may struggle to say "no" — even if they vehemently disagree with you.

When talking to a passive communicator, you might try engaging them on an individual basis, as they may be more comfortable sharing their opinion in private rather than in front of a group. You could also try asking them specific questions that will force them to answer in a manner that goes beyond offering simple "yes" or "no" responses. In essence, it might take some work to draw information out of a tight-lipped passive communicator, so be patient during your interactions with one.

Style 2: Aggressive

Aggressive communicators are loud and proud. They will share their ideas and feelings, even if no one asks for their opinion. They tend to take control of conversations and often don't have the courtesy to let others speak after the discourse is underway. They can also make use of extended eye contact or invade personal space during an argument, all in an effort to pressure others via physical intimidation.

When talking with such an employee, it's important to remain calm and professional. You don't want to escalate the situation by reacting to their hostility with even more hostility. Stand your ground, but do so respectfully. Use assertive language while still empathizing with their viewpoint. Maintain clear boundaries and make sure your point gets across at the close of the exchange.

Style 3: Passive-Aggressive

Passive-aggressive people often seem polite on the surface. But underneath, they can harbor feelings of deep resentment. Their discontentment is often communicated indirectly via subtle comments, sarcasm, or non-verbal cues. It can be challenging to interact with a passive-aggressive communicator because their conniving ways might cause you to second-guess their motives.

When dealing with such a person, always stay calm and composed, addressing each issue directly in a clear and precise manner that leaves little room for obfuscation. Encourage the employee to speak honestly about their concerns. Make it obvious to them that, on your team, it's okay to express constructive disagreement. If you can establish an environment where trust and openness are valued, then you might succeed in ridding the passive-aggressive employee of their need to engage in such acerbic discourse.

Style 4: Assertive

Assertive communication is often viewed as the most effective style that leaders might utilize when talking to their staff. Assertive bosses express their thoughts directly. They speak with confidence, maintain eye contact, use open body language, and respond in a decisive manner. If you happen to have an employee who is also an assertive communicator, then it's important to match their level of clarity and directness. Remain vigilant in conveying your instructions but strive to listen carefully to what they might have to say. If there are disagreements that need addressing, try to keep the dialogue constructive, ensuring that your mutual objective is to arrive at the best solution for the problem, not just to "win" the argument.

As a leader, it's your responsibility to understand and adapt to the communication style of each member of the team. There is no one-size-fits-all solution for effective communication with each employee. People are diverse. Their preferred method of discourse is shaped by their unique experiences, cultural backgrounds, personalities, and values. These characteristics can affect how they perceive messages and how they process incoming data. Your ability to recognize these differences and tailor your communication style accordingly will greatly impact your ability to communicate effectively.

How to communicate firmly, but without aggression

In the previous section, we described how the *assertive* style of communication is often the default style for the leadership role. However, it is important to not confuse assertive discourse with aggressive behavior. The two are not the same. The first major difference is in the way we display our emotions. Ideally, the boss's assertiveness should come packaged with positivity and respect. Aggression, on the other hand, is negative, disrespectful, and physically threatening to the receiving party. The line between the two modes of discourse can be a blurry one. A leader who is assertive (yet constructive) should:

- Be authentic in her opinions and desires
- Be ready to compromise
- Be able to say "no" with tact
- Have clear boundaries and expectations for her employees
- Manage her emotions, never letting *anger* enter a conversation
- Provide honest and constructive feedback
- Cultivate healthy relationships and allies

- Seek out opportunities for collaboration

As a boss, it's all too easy to come off as sounding *aggressive* rather than *assertive*. Hitting the right note sometimes requires a repertoire of verbal acrobatics to achieve. In the proceeding section, I've listed a few communication tactics that you might consider employing when conversing with your staff.

Tactic 1: Use "I" Statements

In conversation, it's easy to use the word "you" in an accusatory manner, as in:

- You said you'd return the stapler an hour ago.
- You were supposed to be here at three o'clock.
- You promised that these documents would be ready after the lunch break.

Instead of overusing the "you" word, consider replacing it with more "I" words, as in:

- "I noticed the stapler hasn't been returned yet."
- "I was expecting your arrival at three o'clock."
- "I was under the impression that we would review that document after lunch."

The latter three statements still sound assertive. But they don't come packaged with an aggressive finger-wagging accusation like the former three statements do. Using "I" statements helps express your perspective without putting the listener on the defensive. This is a more constructive approach, fostering open dialogue and minimizing potential conflicts.

Tactic 2: Negative inquiry

Negative inquiry entails the use of questions to discover exactly what someone means when they cite a disparity. For example, if an employee states that they are not being treated fairly in the office, consider asking probing questions like, "Can you clarify how I've been treating you unfairly?" Or, "Can you provide a specific example of when you were treated unfairly?" Try to get the employee to elaborate on their feelings and perceptions without getting defensive or dismissive. This tactic can help reveal if there's a valid concern that needs to be addressed or if the employee's opinion of the situation is biased. Ideally, by getting the employee to note the specific instances of workplace malevolence, you can begin to unravel the quagmire and find the source of the office friction.

Tactic 3: Fogging

This technique is useful when a coworker is using criticism as a way to manipulate or provoke a reaction from you. Instead of responding defensively, the "fogging" tactic advises us to agree with some aspect of their rant, all while secretly disavowing the rest. For instance, suppose a staff member says, "You never listen to any of my ideas during meetings!" Rather than attempt to refute this claim outright, you might reply by saying, "You're right. There may have been times when I didn't give your ideas the attention they deserved."

This tactic acknowledges their feelings without admitting total fault or blaming the other person. It's called "fogging" because the smokescreen created by this strategy prevents your assailant from identifying a single target to attack. This can throw the other person off their game, hopefully granting you enough time to deescalate the situation and move the conversation along into more productive territory.

Tactic 4: Negative Assertion

This technique involves acknowledging your mistakes or flaws without becoming defensive in your retort. Here, you attempt to own up to your errors and accept that everyone (including you) makes mistakes sometimes. For example, if someone accuses you of being late, you might respond with, "You are correct. There have been times when I've been late. I am actively working to improve my time management skills." This approach allows you to concede the negative aspects of your behavior while also expressing your commitment to personal growth. Our aim is to disarm the criticizer and prevent the conversation from devolving into a confrontation. It also promotes a culture of openness and honesty, as you are showing a willingness to improve upon your shortcomings.

Tactic 5: The Broken Record

This tactic can be useful when facing a particularly irate coworker or customer. Here, the speaker utilizes *repetition* to indicate a refusal to change an opinion. For example, if a customer asks for an unwarranted refund on a product, you can decline stating, "I'm sorry, but I won't be able to accept this product in that condition, as it violates the usage agreement." If the person persists and continues their rant, then (like a broken record) you can repeat the statement: "I'm sorry, but I won't be able to accept this product in that condition, as it violates the usage agreement." People usually get the hint after the second chant. Of course, this sort of passive-aggressive retort should be used sparingly and is generally reserved for de-escalation situations where other communication tactics have proven unsuccessful.

How to practice Active Listening

Your ability to communicate with confidence and competence hinges upon your ability to listen effectively. The role of leadership often calls upon us to exercise our listening skills more than our talking skills. The American psychologists Carl Rogers and Richard Farson introduced the concept of "active listening" in 1957. In their book, Rogers and Farson argued that the most effective way to influence another person is to first understand his mind. They posited that more meaningful connections could be stimulated if each party took a moment to strive for a deeper level of engagement during the conversation. So, what is *active listening*?

- Active listening is listening with conscious intent.
- Active listening entails being fully engaged during the discourse.
- The goal of active listening is *understanding*.

When we're *really* listening to someone, we do much more than merely hear their words and wait for our turn to respond. Instead, we absorb every channel by which they broadcast their intentions. From their vocal tonality to their facial expressions, the data-rich display that emanates from each individual is a reflection of their spirit and their true intentions. Your ability to adequately receive this incoming information will determine your capacity to respond in a way that is empathetic, meaningful, and effective.

As a boss or a leader, our intent is to converse with our employees in a manner that fosters understanding and establishes a clear line of communication from which constructive thoughts and ideas can be exchanged. Hopefully, by electing to approach each conversation with the goal of *active listening* in mind, we can engender a sense of belonging and mutual understanding within each employee. Let's discuss some active listening tips now.

Tip 1: Understand the purpose of the conversation before it starts

Often, we dive into conversations without ever thinking about what we hope to achieve from the discourse. Ideally, we should approach each conversation with an endgame in mind. Of course, given the chaotic nature of business, this is not always possible. Some conversations must emerge spontaneously throughout the business day. However, when we can, it's good to take a moment to envision a positive outcome for the conversation. Ask yourself, "What is my goal in conducting this exchange?"

- To gather information?
- To make a decision?
- To nurture a relationship?
- To persuade a coworker?
- To solve a problem?

By clarifying your purpose beforehand, you can steer the conversation in the right direction and make an effort to ensure that the rendezvous is constructive.

Tip 2: Pay attention to your employee

This tip might sound obvious. But in our modern world of mobile devices and digital distractions, we all know how difficult it is to fully focus on a single task. When we hear the siren song of our chirping cellphone, our attention is spirited away to another dimension, all at the expense of the person sitting before us. Active listening calls upon us to do the opposite. When conversing with an employee, it's important to be fully *present*—not just physically in the room but also mentally engaged.

- Put your smartphone in your desk drawer.
- Close your laptop lid.
- Direct your gaze toward your interlocutor.
- Take note of non-verbal cues—like her facial expressions, her body language, and the tone of her voice.

In doing so, you signal to your employee that you value their words and that you genuinely care about their input. Giving her your undivided attention builds a foundation of trust and respect, both of which can facilitate the smooth conveyance of information.

Tip 3: Be open to learning

Every person you engage with has the capacity to teach you something. That doesn't mean that they will. But it does mean that we should enter every conversation with an open mind. This has two effects.

- First, by seeking to understand your employee's ideas, emotions, or opinions, you will be better equipped to apply the knowledge successfully should the exchange prove useful.
- Second, it just might be the case that their course of action is superior to your own. Part of being confident is being able to admit when you're wrong or when you don't adequately understand something. By valuing diverse

perspectives, you communicate to your staff that their insights are appreciated, and you open yourself up to the prospect of continuous improvement.

Tip 4: Be patient and avoid interrupting

For many of us, this is the most difficult part of being an *active listener*. The urge to interrupt can sometimes be overwhelming. But it's important that we fight it. Whether you're listening to someone rant along a rabbit trail of bad ideas, or spout a personal opinion about a topic you strongly disagree with, it's important to grant your employee an opportunity to speak their piece. By doing so, you indicate that you respect them enough to let their voice be heard. Additionally, being patient and curtailing your interruptions also sets the standard for them to do the same when it's your turn to talk. Hence, when it's time for your retort, you will be more likely to garner the same caliber of respect.

Tip 5: Don't hog the limelight

We've all had the experience of participating in a conversation that devolved into a monologue. Such exchanges can feel more like lectures than dialogues. Participants in the discourse may be quick to tune out—their attention waning and their thoughts wandering away from the topic at hand. If you're in a leadership position, you might feel tempted to try and monopolize every conversation, believing that your status or expertise justifies your claim of the center stage. However, this approach is largely counterproductive. People want to feel heard and valued, and a one-sided conversation might only give way to resentment. Instead, strive for inclusive conversations.

- Ask open-ended questions

- Poll the room for opinions
- Invite people to brainstorm
- Keep your own responses brief when appropriate
- And, show appreciation for all forms of feedback

Not every conversation is a teachable moment. Not every meeting is an opportunity for you to stand on your soapbox and expound on your wisdom. By consciously stepping back and surrendering the floor to other employees, you're signaling to your staff that they are important to the collective effort.

How to give constructive feedback

As a leader, it's important to let the people you're leading know your opinion about which tasks they're currently doing well and which tasks they might improve upon. These conversations can be challenging for new bosses, who often fear that their feedback (especially when it is of a critical nature) may hurt team morale or negatively impact their relationships with subordinates. However, constructive feedback is vital for the growth of both the individual and the team. If you don't attempt to improve your office processes, then your organization will stall, and business development will halt. Below, I've listed a few tips that should help you to provide constructive feedback to your team.

1. **Don't be quick to volunteer unsolicited advice.** Tactless bosses are prone to providing immediate feedback with little or no warning. Sometimes this can't be avoided. But be wary of such spontaneous bursts. Receiving critique is a delicate affair involving higher levels of cognitive processing. Just as each weightlifter needs to warm up his muscles before attempting a deadlift, each employee

ought be given some sort of preamble before being asked to absorb any incoming censure.

2. **Be specific**. No one likes vague feedback. Without concrete examples, the feedback might be rejected, and the learning opportunity will be lost. Hence, when giving constructive criticism, make sure you are clear about what the problems are and exactly what the employee can do to remedy them. The same rule applies when you're providing positive feedback. Don't just say, "Good job." Instead, say, "You did a good job handling that last page of the Robertson report." The specificity of the latter sentence provides the employee with more information about which part of her work she's excelling at.

3. **Keep it private**. No one likes being criticized in public. Some people don't want to be praised in public either. So be conscious of your employees' sensitivities and of the particular group dynamics at play in the workspace. It's usually best to provide negative feedback in a private setting where individuals can feel safe expressing their opinions and feelings without the pressure of being judged by their peers.

4. **"Don't make a sandwich."** A common piece of managerial advice dictates that bosses should deliver bad news between two bits of good news. This is sometimes called a "compliment sandwich." While the intent of this tactic is admirable, its effectiveness is questionable. When asked, most employees would prefer their boss to simply deliver the feedback in a direct and honest fashion. This approach allows them to clearly understand the areas that need improvement without being confused or distracted by the perfunctory compliments—which mostly only serve to waste everyone's time.

5. **Focus on the performance, not the person**. When giving feedback, it's important to avoid attacking the character or personality of the employee. Instead, note the precise behavior that is causing the problem. This means avoiding sentences that start with the word "you" and, instead, focusing on the situation at hand, offering direct examples of instances where the problematic behavior occurred.

The preceding tips should allow you to give feedback that is impactful, well-received, and constructive. Of course, not everyone is going to respond to censure with a spirit of optimism and goodwill. Criticism can be challenging to tolerate, even for mild-mannered people. And yet, as a boss or a leader, it is your responsibility to guide your team towards continuous improvement, not perpetual stagnation. We can only improve if we are aware of our weaknesses and if we make a concerted effort to transform these weaknesses into strengths.

Ch. 6: How to overcome self-doubt and imposter syndrome

When I started my own business, I was terrified before making almost every single decision. I couldn't shake the feeling that I just wasn't ready yet, that I didn't know what I was doing, and that every choice I made would be a bad one. The anxiety was crippling, sometimes paralyzing. Every time I received praise or recognition, I dismissed it as a result of luck or timing, not my own competence.

One day, I was sitting in my office when I received a phone call. It was a client I had been trying to land for weeks. They made us an offer and told me I had until the end of the day to let them know my decision. That might sound great, but the offer wasn't exactly what I had imagined. The timeframe had been moved up from what I had initially suggested, and the payment had been lowered. The gig was still a good opportunity for us as a company. But I knew it would be incredibly difficult to fulfill the contract as presented.

I called my team together and explained the situation. Unfortunately, after describing the problem, there was only silence in the room. I could see everyone trying to process what they'd heard. Eventually, one of my longtime employees looked at me and said, "You're the boss. We'll stick with you no matter what the decision is."

I was speechless. As I looked around the room, I saw nods and smiles. Even though only one person said anything, I saw that I had the full support of my team. I had come into the meeting expecting a unanimous plea to retreat from the offer, thus freeing my staff from the grueling weeks of labor that would result. But I left the meeting with something far more profound: a renewed sense of self-confidence and the realization that I had the full trust of my team. They weren't waiting for me to consult with them but to *lead* them.

I returned to my office, called the client, and refused their initial offer. But I made a counteroffer with a less pressing deadline so I could give my team some more time to labor through the task. The client wasn't happy about the increased wait time. But they had worked with us before, and they eventually agreed to the new terms.

When I put the phone down, I felt like the most powerful woman on Earth. I savored my employee's feedback, "You're the boss." And it was at that moment that I realized I would no longer allow crippling self-doubt to hinder the growth of my company nor my development as a business leader.

Combating Self-Doubt

Why do we doubt ourselves?

Your lower brain utilizes the emotions of doubt, anxiety, and fear to ensure that you don't attempt to do anything that doesn't have a high probability of resulting in a positive outcome. Such angst-ridden agitations of the mind can be readily summoned if you simply think about engaging in a risky venture.

- Would you like to try base jumping from your office building?
- Why not bet all your life savings on a roulette wheel in Las Vegas?
- Have you ever tried to ski with a blindfold on?

If your mind prompts you to doubt your ability to successfully accomplish each one of these activities, then that means your mind is working correctly. Doubt keeps us safe and alive. However, as the adage states:

Your brain exists to help you survive, not to thrive.

If we never take any risk at all, then we would never spread our wings and flee the comfort of our familial nest. To thrive, we need to confront our fears, stretch our boundaries, and (occasionally) engage in calculated risks.

Self-doubts are typically born from negative past experiences. These stinging memories leave a deep imprint upon our minds. And each time we engage in a similar activity, the wound reopens, prompting us to reconsider our course of action. Additionally, our mind is programmed to experience self-doubt when it encounters a novel situation. Though no negative stimulus may be associated with the interaction, your mind's default stance is to avoid any scenario that it's not familiar with, thus keeping you out of the way of any potential harm.

For me, the engine of my self-doubt revved into motion whenever I would compare myself to others. Such comparisons are not always an unhealthy undertaking. Evaluating your success relative to that of another person might help to illuminate the areas in your life that still need improvement. Over time, however, I caught myself gawking at my coworker's success in a way that was not constructive. Instead of seeing their accomplishments as a goalpost to strive for, I saw them as an unreachable standard—one that I was innately incapable of attaining.

These sorts of thoughts are unproductive. Though doubt (like hunger) is a natural faculty of the human experience, we mustn't succumb to its undermining effects. Doubt can be a valuable tool, warning us of possible danger ahead. But, when it prevents us from taking action and realizing our true potential, then it ceases to be helpful and instead becomes a debilitating obstacle.

Here I've listed some tips that have helped me to combat self-doubt and nurture a more confident outlook for my leadership journey.

Tip 1: Set realistic standards

No one is perfect, nor should we try to be. However, as leaders (and even more so as women), we often levy incredibly high expectations upon ourselves. By trying to live up to these unrealistic standards, we set ourselves up for failure. So, consider setting your standards to a level that is realistic and attainable. Recall that the fourth attribute of the SMART goals technique (as discussed in Chapter 3) calls upon us to select a "Realistic" goal. Doing so will enable you to pursue a gradual course of self-development that will prevent you from getting frustrated by the length of the journey that lies before you.

Tip 2: Stop being a "people pleaser"

I've seen many businesswomen struggle to pursue their business objectives while still trying to please all the people around them. They refused to disappoint their staff, family, children, and friends. And they would go to herculean efforts to make sure everyone was satisfied. Like most women who have had the fortune of being both a boss and a mother, I too have been quick to fall into the "people pleaser" role. But, as the saying goes:

You can please some of the people all of the time.
You can please all of the people some of the time.
But you can't please all of the people all of the time.

Our quest to keep everyone happy inevitably ends in failure. You don't have enough hands to meet everyone's expectations forever. Moreover, persisting in this mission can lead to exhaustion and burnout—which are quick to give way to the feelings of inadequacy and self-doubt that we were trying to avoid in the first place. Instead of falling into this viscous cycle, focus on defining and nurturing a finite set of your most vital priorities and values. It's okay to say "no" to things that don't align with your goals. By trying to please everyone, you'll only end up pleasing no one, including yourself.

Tip 3: Celebrate little victories

When we're struggling with self-doubt, it's important to celebrate every little victory. Doing so creates reference experiences in the mind. The more your lower mind is convinced that your actions will result in positive gains, the less it will try to dissuade you from engaging in uncertain business endeavors in the future.

Thus, take a moment to celebrate when you complete a new objective. Your festivities need not be a lavish affair. You don't have to have an office party every time you get a new client. Keep things simple. When a new minor milestone has been won, try closing your eyes for a moment and listen for the sound of fortune's call.

- Take a deep breath.
- Let your mind acknowledge your hard work and the effort it took to traverse this stint of the journey.
- Recognize the progress you've made and allow yourself to feel proud of it.
- And then, return to the grindstone and get back to work.

These little rituals not only act as positive reinforcement for our productive behaviors, they also help to create a more optimistic mindset. By focusing on the positive gains made at each step of the journey, you can focus your perspective on the benefits to be had on the road ahead. Doing so assuages your emotional mind and makes the intrusive feelings of self-doubt more manageable.

Tip 4: Establish a growth mindset

A "growth mindset" (the belief that one's abilities can be developed and improved over time) lies in contrast to a "fixed mindset," which posits that our talents are innate and static. A person who has adopted a growth mindset has taught herself to perceive the world in a certain way.

- She embraces challenges and sees them (not as setbacks) but as opportunities for growth.

- She understands that failure is part of the process. Each stumble is merely a single datapoint that can be utilized to divulge more information about the path we must walk.
- She knows that one's education never stops. And that innovation is a gift bestowed upon those who are hungry and curious.
- She knows that the journey is the destination. And that the process is to be valued more than the riches promised to us at the end of the trek.

If you can learn to approach each endeavor with a growth mindset, then each impediment to your success need not be perceived as a confirmation of your ineptitude nor as an excuse to engage in self-doubt. Instead, such setbacks are merely opportunities to keep improving and persevering. This is what the leadership role demands of us.

Tip 5: You don't have to "have it all" to be successful

As I mentioned earlier in this book, there came a point in my life when I decided I wanted a family *and* a career. However, there also came a point when I simply couldn't maintain the standards that I was trying to live up to in both domains. I tried to be everything my heroes were. If I couldn't do it all (like they seemingly could), then that must mean I'm not a very good leader, mother, or businessperson. But after running on this treadmill for a while, I realized I was on the fast track to burnout.

While some people in this world seem to be endowed with the gift of *industriousness*, not everyone should aspire to pursue a similar life strategy. The formula that allows some of our ilk to achieve outlier levels of success is a mysterious one—even to the businesspeople who have obtained such impressive heights. You can spend a lifetime trying to crack the code, and you still might never find it. Hence, it's best to not become so blinded by the vision of where you'd like to be, that you forget to make the most of where you are now.

Canceling Imposter Syndrome

In their 1978 paper titled *"The Impostor Phenomenon in High Achieving Women,"* researchers Pauline Clance and Suzanne Imes reported on their observation that many high-achieving women harbored a belief that they were *frauds* and not worthy of the academic or financial success they had achieved. This belief seemed to persist no matter how many credentials or accolades the women managed to accrue.

This pattern of thought, now commonly known as *"impostor syndrome,"* is defined as:

The persistent refusal to believe that one's success is deserved or that it has been achieved legitimately, i.e., as a result of one's labor, intelligence, or skill.

Women with impostor syndrome tend to attribute their success to luck or timing, rather than to their own competence or capabilities. Oddly, even high-performing women who have substantial external evidence of their high skill level still might find that they are burdened with crippling self-doubt.

The opposite of a belief in one's *incompetence* is a belief in one's *self-efficacy*. In psychology, self-efficacy is defined as:

A person's belief in their ability to successfully pursue a course of action that is necessary to produce a desired outcome.

In other words, someone with a high degree of *self-efficacy* believes in their ability to accomplish tasks, overcome challenges, and achieve new goals. Their mental fortitude influences their mental state, allowing them to remain resilient and approach new setbacks with optimism. In contrast, a woman with a *low* sense of self-efficacy shies away from risky situations. If the task is difficult, she might doubt her ability to rise to the occasion and complete the objective. But even if she is successful in her endeavors, she may not be fully convinced that her victory was the result of her prowess. When these bouts of self-doubt begin to permeate her thoughts and interrupt her workday, then she is said to be suffering from *imposter syndrome*.

Obviously, we'd all like to be endowed with a belief in our own *self-efficacy* rather than burdened with the nausea of *self-doubt*. So, how can we prompt our minds to engender the former emotion over the latter? In this section, we'll discuss some tips to make that happen.

Tip 1: Be competent

Ashlee Vance's biography on Elon Musk is full of stories portraying Musk's mindboggling commitment to his work. Vance noted a story conveyed by one of Musk's early employees who stated:

> **[Elon] never seemed to leave the office. He slept, not unlike a dog, on a beanbag next to his desk. Almost every day, I'd come in at seven thirty or eight A.M., and he'd be asleep right there on that bag... Maybe he showered on the weekends. I don't know. [Elon would ask his] employees ... to give him a kick when they arrived, and he'd wake up and get back to work.**

Perhaps the best "management technique" you can utilize to convince yourself (and your employees) to trust in your competence is to simply become the most competent or hardest-working person in the room. This entails being on time, being organized, being consistent, and putting in long hours at the office. This means arriving at the workplace before everyone else does, and leaving the workplace after everyone has gone home.

This is not to say that you must be able to do the job of every staff member, nor that you must be the smartest person in the room. (I'm convinced that most of my employees have a much higher IQ than me.) But when your employees witness such displays of conscientiousness and stick-to-itiveness, they will be more inclined to trust you to make the right decision, Or, in the least, if they see that you're willing to work harder on the problem than anyone else, then they should be more likely to believe in your ability to find a solution. Garnering the respect of your team in this fashion will prompt your subconscious mind to believe that you are worthy of your role, and all the success that comes along with it.

Tip 2: Review your achievements

While we should all strive to remain humble about our personal abilities and skillset, it's proper to take an occasional moment to acknowledge past victories. Everyone has overcome a challenge of some sort. Everyone has faced a scuffle in which they emerged the victor. Maintaining a log of such triumphs, and reviewing them thoroughly, can be invaluable on the days when the echoes of self-doubt are particularly strident in the hollows of your mind. This corpus of victories might be stored in a scrapbook, a computer folder, or in a diary. Regardless of the medium, it's healthy to revisit your past accomplishments from time to time.

Why?

Because it's quite easy to spot your own shortcomings. It's quite easy to stare into the mirror and note each little flaw. But it's also easy to forget how far you have come, and how many successes you have already won in your life. By reliving such moments, we hope to reignite the spark of confidence that you experienced after achieving victory—that little blast of dopamine that is released in your brain each time you succeed in completing a new goal.

Tip 3: Understand that you're not alone

It's hard to put a number on exactly how many women suffer from imposter syndrome. This is complicated by the fact that we all experience self-doubt from time to time. So, it can be difficult to discern when these natural misgivings have become pathological. One study performed by KPMG at their *Women's Leadership Summit* in 2020 found that 75% of women in executive positions have struggled with imposter syndrome at some point in their careers. Hence, if you're a woman in a leadership position, and you find that notions of self-doubt reverberate through your skull more often than you'd like, just know that you're not alone. These misgivings are common. You need not worry about such reflexive fears any more than you would worry about your fear of heights. Just accept such reservations for what they are—perturbations of the mind that are designed to prevent you from engaging in risky behavior. But if the risks you take are *calculated risks*, then there is no reason to give in to such disruptive thoughts.

Tip 4: Note which workplace events trigger your anxiety

Don't try to deny your emotions when you're experiencing self-doubt. Suppressing these feelings might only serve to amplify them. Instead, take note of the set of stimuli that tends to trigger your feelings of inadequacy in the workplace.

- Do you tense up at the thought of releasing your next product?
- Do you put off looking at your financial statements because the minuscule profit margins make you queasy?
- Do you avoid meeting with peers in your industry because you don't want to discuss any work-related struggles?

Whatever the triggers might be, acknowledging them is the first step to managing them. Consider keeping a log of stimuli that prompted you to feel inadequate. Note the emotions that ensued and the thoughts you had during this episode. Hopefully, as your log grows, you'll be able to spot patterns in your data. And you'll know which situations are most likely to incite such feelings of self-doubt. Understanding these triggers will allow you to mentally prepare yourself for any upcoming social situation in which such an episode is likely to re-occur. This way, if the situation incites such angst-ridden emotions, you will at least be prepared for them, and their potential impact upon your mental state will be lessened.

Tip 5: Find a mentor or a confidant

Even the titans of industry need a shoulder to cry on every once in a while. Simply talking about your doubts and fears has a funny way of making them seem less intimidating. Hence, it's vital that you find a mentor or a confidant that is willing to listen to your woes. Ideally, this person will be someone who has experienced the same caliber of work-related strife. And who can provide guidance, feedback, and reassurance about your ability to navigate the road ahead.

Tip 6: It's ok to admit that you don't have all the answers

One of the hallmarks of a woman with impostor syndrome is her belief that she must have an answer to every question that comes across her desk. This, of course, is an unattainable standard. No one knows it all. So don't try to pretend you do. Instead of viewing a gap in your knowledge as a weakness, learn to see it as an opportunity for growth. People have much more respect for someone who honestly concedes a lack of knowledge about a particular topic than a person who feigns expertise. Admitting that you don't have all the answers demonstrates intellectual humility. Indicating that you are willing to pursue the answer to a question with more rigor than anyone else in the room exhibits that you're trying to discover the best course of action for the good of the team.

So, do not fear that familiar twinge of angst that arises when a new obstacle presents itself. Just as your muscles can only grow when they encounter a stressor, so too is your personal confidence subject to the same laws of the cosmos. This is what we mean when we recite Friedrich Nietzsche's oft-cited mantra:

What doesn't kill me makes me stronger.

The path to growth (both personal and professional) often involves meeting challenges head-on and fearlessly pushing through the fog of doubt—that thick miasma that forever seems intent on dissuading us from progressing along the path of success. That resistance you feel may just be an indication that you're on the cusp of a metamorphosis. And, as each new version of yourself emerges, the spirits of doubt will be less likely to haunt your thoughts and dissuade you from continuing along your journey.

Ch. 7: How to make your feminine energy work for you

It's taken the business world a long time to realize the value of female traits like empathy, intuition, and emotional intelligence. In the past, conventionally female faculties have been viewed as *weaknesses* rather than *assets*. But the companies that have embraced such diverse skills have begun to reap the rewards. In this book, we've examined how you might go about manifesting traits that are typically associated with masculine energy—like assertiveness, ambition, and a willingness to take risks. But women are often too quick to deride the virtues of feminine energy in the workplace—possibly because so many of us feel an overwhelming pressure to "fit in" and "hang with the boys."

I've sat through many seminars and speeches led by women in business. Invariably, the majority of them downplay the role of feminine energy in favor of traditional masculine roles. The focus in such presentations tends to revolve around concepts like:

- How to be more aggressive.
- How to drive a harder bargain.
- How to appear more assertive.
- How to get what you want.

Each one of these pursuits is important in the business world. And we should all strive to tap into a more masculine persona when appropriate. But, in doing so, we must not forget the value of *diplomacy* or *adaptability*. As Bruce Lee advised, when we encounter an obstacle, the best strategy might be to:

> **...be like water making its way through cracks... Adjust to the object, and you shall find a way around or through it.**

As women, we should remain aware of the alternate repertoire of tactics that we have at our disposal. Feminine energy is not about being weak. It's about using our innate graces to foster collaboration, nurture growth, and create a space where each employee feels welcomed and motivated to contribute at their highest possible potential. In this chapter, we're going to take a deep dive into the power of feminine energy in the workplace. We'll discuss how it differs from the masculine, how it can be leveraged for better business outcomes, and why it is such a critical factor if we are to manage the complexities of a 21st-century labor force.

What is Male and Female Energy?

We don't have to choose between feminine and masculine energy. We all possess elements of both. Note that every battery has a positive and a negative terminal. They wouldn't be able to function without each one. Our core energy operates in a similar manner. And, though we may lean toward one over the other, it's best to embrace *both* forms if we are to become the best leader we can be.

- A male leader who empathizes with young employees and strives to engender the spirits of collaboration among his staff, might be said to be "embracing his feminine energy."

- A female leader who is audacious and assertive in the boardroom has traditionally been labeled as having "masculine energy."

Regardless of how antiquated this categorization exercise might seem, it is a fixture of biology that is unlikely to dissipate anytime soon. There is a time and a place for both identities to take center stage. And there is value in our ability to recognize, understand, and portray such dualistic facets of our personalities at will. As Lao Tzu wrote:

Knowing others is wisdom, knowing yourself is Enlightenment.
Mastering others is strength, mastering yourself is true power.
He who embraces unity becomes the universe's self.

We're often taught that, in order to "make it in a man's world," we need to be aggressive, driven, logical, and unemotional. These are the prototypical traits of masculine energy. However, while there is a time and a place for such audacious displays, we need not conclude that they comprise *all* the ingredients needed for a workplace to function. New female bosses often make the mistake of trying to extinguish the spark of feminine energy that burns within them, believing that to display any form of perceived vulnerability might weaken their image. But we need not view feminine energy as such a liability. Embracing it can bring about a multitude of strengths and benefits which could be described by many adjectives. Women are:

- Creative
- Compassionate
- Connected
- Patient
- Empathetic
- Reflective
- Inspirational
- Intuitive
- Nurturing
- Collaborative
- Adaptable

Every alpha needs an omega. The *feminine* need not be the antithesis of the *masculine*. Instead, it can be its compliment. As should be obvious, our preceding list of traits has great utility in the contemporary workplace, useful for attracting loyal employees and maintaining long-lasting relationships within the organization. In many offices, feminine energy seems to have a magnetic power—acting as an invisible force that binds employees together despite their abrasive exterior.

- It promotes the idea of teamwork and collective success over individual triumphs.
- It notes the benefit of raw intelligence as well as emotional intelligence.
- It doesn't strive to seek dominion over each member of a corporate hierarchy, but to harmonize the efforts of every employee.

While some might dismiss these qualities as being "too soft," I believe them to be just as crucial to business success as conventionally masculine traits. If a leader manages to harness both energies concomitantly, she will be better able to respond to the diverse needs and motivations of each team member, adopting a holistic approach to problem-solving that takes into account both the logic-driven (masculine) and the relationship-oriented (feminine) variables that comprise the formula of success.

Remember, this isn't necessarily about gender. Both men and women are capable of manifesting the energies of each other. Instead, it's about understanding the unique strengths that each energy brings to the boardroom, and leveraging them effectively to create a balanced leadership style. Below, we'll discuss how you might tap into the feminine side of your workplace persona.

How to Leverage Your Feminine Energy

Tip 1: Embrace Creativity in the Workplace

Given today's dynamic business landscape, creativity is no longer an indulgence; it's a necessity. Mankind has long associated creative energy with feminine energy. In Greek mythology, the nine daughters of Zeus and Mnemosyne were referred to as "The Muses." They are the goddesses of literature, art, and science. As women, we have a natural desire to express ourselves via some form of creative outlet. Many of us are at our best when we're able to tap into our creative side. Whether you're brainstorming novel marketing ideas or designing a new product line, creative thinking is the key that unlocks workplace innovation.

Embracing the spirits of creativity is not merely an undertaking for graphic artists or product designers. Every facet of industry can benefit from an artful approach to problem-solving. Employees who can *think outside the box* are more likely to stumble upon serendipitous solutions. Leaders who aim to cultivate such an environment must create a culture that encourages curiosity and tolerates failure. This is vital; because most *moonshots* fail. In the business world, a *moonshot* is defined as:

An ambitious, exploratory project that is undertaken without any expectation of immediate profitability, but with the hope of achieving a novel breakthrough that will lead to future success.

Cultivating an environment where creativity is valued (and risks are encouraged) may lead to fortuitous outcomes that can propel the company into lofty realms of success. Leaders who are open to experimentation recognize that innovation doesn't typically result from the pursuit of immediate gains but from the exploration of uncharted territories.

Tip 2: Collaborate with your Team

To paraphrase Aristotle:

The whole is greater than the sum of its parts.

As business leaders, we know that when each employee in the company is connected and working together in concert, then the resultant output of this synergy is much greater than the minuscule output that any single individual can hope to achieve. For this reason, collaboration and teamwork are the cornerstones on which the success of the organization must rest. Women are particularly well suited for this endeavor because we come equipped with a high degree of social acuity. Our charms are famous for their ability to resolve tensions and bring people together. And we're more naturally endowed with the traits of *empathy* and *understanding*—which are necessary for any leader that wishes to summon the spirits of collaboration.

Tip 3: Practice Empathetic Communication

In Chapter 5, we discussed the value of active listening, which calls upon the practitioner to engage deeply with the speaker—tuning in to the words they utter, but also to the underlying emotions and intentions conveyed via the subtle nuances of the discourse. Women are better at reading people than men. We know how to "read between the lines." We take note of the unspoken concerns that float under the ether of a conversation. In a world dominated by raw data, the human element of business negotiation is often overlooked. This is unfortunate since alliances are achieved and relationships are forged, not by machines or organizations but by people. Relationships are the lifeblood of business. Your ability to read, understand, and connect with others on a higher plane of consciousness can set you apart in an otherwise hostile, dog-eat-dog world.

The ability to empathize is an under-appreciated proficiency. Skilled empaths can pick up on the emotional state of anyone in their vicinity. They can effortlessly connect with people, especially during those times when forging a stronger bond would be socially advantageous. A woman's unique ability to read a room—especially one full of bellicose individuals whose interior thoughts and ulterior motives might be questionable in nature—is of obvious benefit in the business world.

Tip 4: Leverage Your Superior Social Skills

Women are typically more social than men. And those who possess superior social skills have a unique ability to navigate the complexities of human relationships with ease. But what are "social skills" exactly?

The term is difficult to codify. But Daniel Goleman (the researcher who popularized *Emotional Intelligence* as discussed in Chapter 1) provides us with a useful definition. He states:

> **[Social skills are not] just a matter of friendliness, although people with high levels of social skill are rarely mean-spirited. Social skill, rather, is *"friendliness with a purpose"* ... [This ability enables you to move] people in the direction you desire, whether that's agreement on a new marketing strategy, or enthusiasm about a new product.**

Your ability to bring about this "friendliness with a purpose" is invaluable in the business world. It's tempting to believe that partnerships are formed and fortunes are made following a rigorous analysis of market conditions and a reasoned discourse that enumerates how all interested parties can benefit from a deal. But, as we all know, this isn't how business actually works. Instead, people usually choose to make a deal with you based simply on *how much they like you.*

The world of white-collar business is one of the many domains in which your social skills really do translate into dollars. If you know how to win the trust and admiration of your colleagues and clients, then doors will forever be opening before you. Social acumen is an invaluable tool that can ease your journey across the rough landscape of the business world. It's about more than mere friendliness; it's about understanding people, recognizing their unique goals, and then aligning your efforts such that your actions benefit all parties involved. All business ventures are fueled by cooperative efforts that result from such interpersonal interactions.

Tip 5: Play to Your Strengths

We all have strengths and weaknesses. The trick to succeeding in any game (football, love, or business) is to first discover the strengths that you (or your team) uniquely possess. And then, to leverage these strengths so that they work to your advantage. In a business context, the phrase "play to your strengths" isn't just about recognizing what you do well. You must also understand how those qualities can be applied to the unique demands of your industry.

Traditionally, the annals of business have been written by men. And hence, each page of history has emphasized the role of masculine strength and energy. This is not necessarily a reflection of the utility of these attributes but rather a product of the societal norms and power dynamics that have festered since the dawn of time. But, as this century unfolds, an intriguing metamorphosis is taking place within the corporate arena. Traditional leadership paradigms are being abandoned. The modern labor force is no longer spurred to action by cigar-chomping fat cats, who stand atop their desk, shouting out commands and whipping their galley slaves to action. Technicians, administrators, and artisans do not respond well to barked orders. Instead, managing the social sensibilities of the modern workplace requires a more nuanced skill—one that women are uniquely positioned to provide. By embracing and playing to these strengths, women have an opportunity to reshape the business landscape and claim more of the territory that has eluded their grasp for far too long.

Ch. 8: How to avoid burnout and maintain a work-life balance

One of my greatest role models is a woman named Meredith. She was one of the C-suite executives at a company that I interned at after college, and I can honestly say that I idolized her. She was the most confident, talented, and caring person I had ever worked with. It took me a couple years to muster up the courage to ask her for some one-on-one advice. But she was happy to comply. One coffee turned into two, and soon we were meeting every month for a full mentoring session. I have learned so much from her over the years that I can't imagine who I would be today without her. I valued those sessions more than any other meeting in my workday. Which is why I was immediately concerned one afternoon when I arrived at our local coffee shop only to find that Meredith wasn't there. She was always early, not just for our appointments, but for social events and dinner functions. I immediately called her cellphone but got no answer. After a couple more tries, I drove to her house. Her husband opened the door and, seeing the panicked look on my face, assured me that everything was being taken care of. Meredith was at a sanctuary, attending a retreat to recover from burnout.

After a month of being away, Meredith finally contacted me, and we met at her home. When I arrived, I had many questions, but I decided to let her speak first. It took her a couple minutes to gather

her thoughts before she began recounting her tale. She had been under such incredible pressure for so long that her mind simply couldn't take it anymore. Her schedule had been full for years. She hadn't taken any time off in over a decade. But one day in April, she couldn't get out of bed. Her husband was certain that something was wrong. They visited their doctor, and he diagnosed her with *burnout*. So, she locked her cellphone away and headed off to a mountain retreat.

After she shared her story with me, I had one burning question, "Why hadn't she told me she was under so much pressure?" The response she squeaked out pains me to this day. "I just don't like to look weak or incompetent in front of anyone," she said.

I was shocked. I realized at that moment how blind I had been to her trauma. During our meetings, I had always inquired about the basics, "How is Jonathan and the kids?" or "How's that big project going?" But I had never dug any deeper than that. And I wondered how many other people in my office were under the same degree of pressure. Maybe the signs were there, but I just wasn't seeing them. If I had been better at reading people, perhaps I would have noticed that something was amiss with my friend and mentor. This incident brought about a profound change in the way I approach my workplace relationships. And it prompted me to delve deeper into the topics of burnout, stress, and the never-ending quest to maintain a healthy work-life balance.

What is Occupational Burnout?

Burnout is a serious issue. Most people in the business world will experience burnout or the symptoms of burnout at some point in their careers. According to the World Health Organization, *occupational burnout* is defined as:

A syndrome ... resulting from chronic workplace stress, that has not been successfully managed.

The three most recognizable symptoms of the illness are:

- *Exhaustion*: Wherein the employee feels overwhelmed, drained, and unable to keep up with the demands of the job. The fatigue resulting from such pressure is chronic, in that the employee constantly feels physically and emotionally depleted.
- *Negativity or Cynicism*: The employee may be unable to pursue workplace activities with a positive demeanor. And may have a cynical attitude during all work-related interactions.
- *Reduced Efficiency*: The employee notices that she's making mistakes on the job, and that she is no longer able to accomplish tasks that were, in the past, handled with ease.

The condition was recognized long ago, even making a brief appearance in the bible. But our current conception of *burnout* is perhaps best attributed to the work of the American psychologist Herbert Freudenberger who, in 1974, wrote an academic paper for the *Journal of Social Issues* in which he discussed the tendency for his hospital staff to "burn-out" after working in a high-stress clinical environment. Freudenberger later went on to outline twelve stages of burnout which we'll surmise here:

- Stage 1: The employee feels the need to prove herself. So, she takes on more responsibilities and pursues lofty goals, all in an effort to demonstrate her worth or increase her financial standing.
- Stage 2: She says "yes" to everything, pledging to do more than she is capable of completing.
- Stage 3: The employee may often neglect her physical needs, skipping mealtime and sleep time just so she can get more done.
- Stage 4: Any problems that might arise within her personal life are disregarded, displaced by work-related tasks that require her immediate attention.
- Stage 5: She may begin to sense that her workload is having a negative effect on her. But she dismisses these inklings in favor of her commitment to increased productivity.
- Stage 6: Her stress might come in the form of workplace aggression in which she perceives her colleagues as working too slowly and belittles them for not keeping up with her pace.
- Stage 7: She withdrawals from her social life. Now, everything is about work.
- Stage 8: Other people in her family begin to notice the changes in her demeanor. In lieu of engaging in healthy social activities, she might turn to alcohol or antidepressants.
- Stage 9: She enters the office each morning in a catatonic state. Her enthusiasm is gone, but her body keeps

working, going through the motions, and trying to complete every assigned task.

- Stage 10: She entertains the idea of quitting or jetting off on a dream vacation someplace warm. She starts to feel as if her work has no meaning.
- Stage 11: She is emotionally and mentally exhausted, and depression begins to take root.
- Stage 12: The employee has burned out. She will eventually have a complete mental or physical breakdown.

It is likely that our preceding list reminds you of someone you know. Perhaps you can even recognize some elements of your own career arc in these twelve stages. Everyone experiences stress at some point in their life. Indeed, stress is a fundamental component of the human experience. Stress is your brain's way of telling you that your attention should be devoted to a perilous situation, and that failure to attend to this situation might be hazardous to your personal safety, financial security, or social standing. Stress is the emotion that kept your ancestors alive. And, while it is true that, in today's world, your failure to complete all the tasks on your to-do list will probably not result in death, your lower mind still feels inclined to produce the same angst-ridden fight-or-flight response that it used to prod your predecessors to action in the Pleistocene.

In this chapter, we'll discuss the underlying causes of stress and burnout. And we'll review some strategies you can employ to foster a healthier work-life balance.

Finding a proper Work-Life Balance

Most of us have heard the term "work-life balance" before. But what does the expression truly mean? And why does the goal of achieving it remain an elusive endeavor for so many?

In a single sentence, maintaining a healthy *work-life balance* might be defined as:

The act of harmonizing one's professional and social responsibilities, such that both endeavors can grow and thrive without detracting from the other.

Our familial and social obligations will always lie in contrast to our professional duties and our financial liabilities. But we must not view these interests as competing antagonists. Instead, we should perceive them as discrete ingredients in a recipe for a well-rounded and fulfilling life. Each goal complements the other. Each pursuit could not exist without the other. And yet, when we try to merge the two domains (e.g., when we attempt to converse with our sister while texting a colleague), then we usually only succeed in diminishing the quality and depth of both interactions.

We've all been there before. We've all heard the chime of our cellphone and felt the lure of the office. When the electronic tones of our modern-day communication devices squeal at us, we hurry to tend to their alarm like a mama bear racing to defend her crying cubs. Have you ever caught yourself doing any of the following:

- Taking work calls during dinnertime
- Checking emails every 30 seconds
- Multitasking during family events

- Bringing reams of work-related paperwork home on Fridays
- Missing family parties because of work commitments
- Feeling guilty when engaging in recreational activities or hobbies
- Allowing the stress of the boardroom to follow you home to the dining room

Obviously, such interruptions are not conducive to our goal of striking a balance between our personal and professional lives. Such habits will only succeed in straining our relationships, engendering feelings of resentment, detachment, and isolation. Given the interconnectedness of our media-saturated world, it's tempting to think that emerging technology enables us to walk and chew gum at the same time. But, as we've all experienced before, we usually just end up tripping over ourselves or biting our lips.

The human brain is not designed for true multitasking, especially when it comes to complex tasks that require focus, emotional intelligence, and deep thinking. In his best-selling productivity book "Deep Work," the computer scientist Cal Newport writes:

If you keep interrupting your evening to … respond to email or put aside a few hours after dinner to catch up on an approaching deadline, you're robbing your directed attention centers of the uninterrupted rest they need for restoration. Even if these work dashes consume only a small amount of time, they prevent you from reaching the levels of "deeper relaxation" in which attention restoration can occur… [To put it] another way, trying to squeeze a little more work out of your evenings might [actually] reduce your effectiveness the next day…

The human brain is not a computer. It's not built for multitasking like your laptop's CPU is. Instead, we usually function at our best when we devote specific tasks to specific domains. These domains go by many names:

- The boardroom
- The office
- The desk
- The parking lot
- The subway
- The bus
- The car
- The gym
- The pool
- The bathroom
- The rocking chair
- The porch
- The kitchen
- The bedroom

Take a moment to note the many different stations that you visit each day. Notice how each station is tooled to perform a specific function. Some of these stations are devoted to work-related tasks, and others exist for recreation, socializing, or personal hygiene. In some of these domains, we chat with colleagues. And in others, we only converse with our confidants. Finding a proper work-life balance means recognizing the great utility to be had when we erect boundaries around each domain—compartmentalizing our behaviors and manifesting a different persona for each interest.

The communication devices of the modern world allow us to transcend the distances that have historically allowed us to bifurcate our concerns. And, though it is true that these mechanical marvels allow for a host of life-saving inventions (the 911 Emergency service for example), it is also the case that they can blur the lines between our *work life* and our *social life* in unhealthy ways. The trick to managing this mayhem is to learn how to harness the benefits of technology while still protecting the privacy of the domains in which it does not belong. This entails eliminating any crosstalk that flows between your work and home. One of the best ways to accomplish this is to ensure that you complete your work-related tasks during work hours. Of course, the most common retort to this conjecture is to simply insist that "there is always more work to do" or that there just "aren't enough hours in the day…" Then, the entrepreneur will cite her demanding schedule and approaching deadlines to evidence her claim, insisting that *time scarcity* is the culprit that is preventing her from achieving a well-balanced life.

While *time* is indeed a finite resource that we must attend to, most of our work-balance issues stem from the inferior way that we manage it. If you don't believe me, try this experiment:

- Tomorrow morning, set a stopwatch to chime every 15 minutes throughout the day.
- Carry a notebook with you and write down the activity you're engaged in each time the 15-minute alarm is sounded.
- When your day is over, take a moment to examine every 15-minute block of time. And then ask yourself, "How efficient was I today?"

Most likely, you'll discover that your time was not utilized as competently as you might have hoped. A typical 24-hour day consists of 16 hours of wakefulness followed by 8 hours of sleep. But ask yourself:

- How many of those 16 hours are devoted to eating, chatting, texting, or browsing the internet?
- How many of those 16 hours do you actually spend "working?"
- And, most importantly, of the hours that you did spend at work, how many of those hours were devoted to doing something impactful?

While most of us do manage to spend eight hours on the office floor each day, most of us are also well aware of the fact that only a fraction of that time is spent doing meaningful labor—i.e., important work that will have a significant impact on our bottom line and push the needle of progress forward. Unfortunately, much of our time is consumed by a mix of administrative tasks, casual social interactions, unnecessary meetings, and unanticipated interruptions. (Not to mention the billions of wasted hours that the national labor force devotes to staring at YouTube and Instagram each year.)

This mismanagement of time is often the main impediment to achieving our coveted work-life balance. For many professionals, it's not so much about working harder but rather about working smarter. For entrepreneurs and business leaders—whose daily tasks often extend above and beyond the usual scope of responsibilities—*task prioritization* is essential to creating a work environment that not only fosters productivity but also respects the boundaries that must exist between our work life and our personal life. Let's discuss some tips that should help you to focus your efforts.

How to focus on your most vital objectives

Tip 1: Start with the "Rule of 3s"

If you're new to the world of personal productivity and time management, then the "Rule of 3s" is a great place to start your training. It advises the practitioner to simply write down three tasks that they'd like to accomplish during the workday. And then to prioritize these tasks above all other intrusions that will inevitably leap onto your desk as the day progresses.

This might sound like an easy venture. Anyone can get three things done. Right?

However, as someone who has been maniacally obsessed with the art of task-tracking for three decades, I can attest to the difficulty of this endeavor. The chaotic exigencies of the office will forever be vying for your attention.

- Emails pour into your inbox at the moment you turn on your computer.
- Coworkers burst through your office doors like busboys at a diner.
- The phone rings incessantly. And the voice on the other end grows increasingly agitated with each passing hour.

It is sometimes hard to believe that, amidst this turmoil, your job is to actually "get stuff done." Getting stuff done is hard. That's why the Rule of 3s has great utility in that it aids in focusing the mind on what truly matters. By narrowing your list of daily objectives to just three primary tasks, you can mitigate the signal-to-noise ratio and focus on the most essential activities that lie in wait amidst the pandemonium of the workplace.

Tip 2: Use the Seven Mudas to identify points of friction.

Within every office, there are points of friction that prevent your workforce from obtaining optimum efficiency. When working for Toyota in the 1960s, the Japanese auto engineer Taiichi Ohno attempted to create a system to catalog each pain point. He termed his taxonomy "The Seven Mudas." In English, the word "muda" means "waste." By identifying these seven wastes within an organization, we can identify unnecessary activities and focus more intently on our most vital objectives. Let's briefly describe each *muda* now.

1. **Wasteful Motion**: Every tool an employee needs to complete her job should be available to her. If she has to stop what she's doing and leave her workstation to complete a daily task, then this lull in activity is probably wasteful.

2. **Wasteful Transportation**: Moving a product costs money. If your product is bouncing between suppliers and distributors, then there may be a problem in your logistical infrastructure.

3. **Wasteful Waiting**: In any workflow, it is often the case that one person cannot do their job until another person is finished. Be careful to spot any hindrances that halt the flow of activity in your office.

4. **Wasteful Over-production**: Producing more products than we need might be costing us money. Strive to properly gauge future demand.

5. **Wasteful Over-processing**: The amount of effort we put into a task is superficial if the target consumer never actually perceives the benefit of our increased labor. Be careful to avoid over-engineering your end product.

6. **Wasteful Inventory**: The longer your product sits unused or unpurchased, the more money it costs you.
7. **Wasteful Defects**: A production line that produces too many duds is a costly one.

You don't need to own an automobile factory to be mindful of the many similar inefficiencies that are quick to infiltrate any work environment. Even the humblest small business is susceptible to the same sorts of resource-wasting hindrances. By understanding and addressing these wastes (these "mudas") team leaders can streamline their business operations, optimizing their team's workflow so that they can become laser-focus on their most critical objectives.

Tip 3: Say "no" to just about everything
Warren Buffett once famously quipped:

The difference between successful people and really successful people is that really successful people say "no" to almost everything.

This entails saying "no" to the typical workplace distractions— like social media, office chatter, and inconsequential emails. But it also means saying "no" to ideas that sound promising—like new marketing strategies, new productivity enhancers, and new feature requests. For a young entrepreneur, learning to say "no" to a potentially promising idea can be torturous. The decision might even gnaw at your brain each night before you drift off to sleep. And you may be haunted by the question of whether pursuing the new course of action would have been superior to sticking to the course you're currently on.

Unfortunately, the road to riches is dotted with many forks. Yes, some roads will get you to El Dorado faster. But the majority of roads lead to Gehenna. As the adage states:

Most pioneers die with arrows in their backs.

Meaning that:

- Most of your business ventures will fail.
- Most new strategies you try will not produce very fruitful results.
- And most of your bright ideas will amount to nothing more than dim memories.

Such is the harsh reality of business innovation. But thankfully, we don't need to successfully execute a million great ideas to make a fortune. To partake in the joys of success, we only need to be right about one or two. This is why it's so important to focus on your *core competencies* and strive to only execute the initiatives that most closely align with your business vision. We must be discerning when selecting which ideas to pursue, and which ones to abandon. Every new project you take on divides your attention, energy, and resources. Though rejecting a seemingly bright idea can be painful, doing so at least ensures that you are not being led astray by distractions. When it comes to achieving significant success in your field, *depth* is usually more crucial than *breadth*. As Steve Jobs said:

People think "focus" means saying "yes" to the thing you've got to focus on. But that's not what it means at all. It means saying "no" to the hundred other good ideas. You have to pick carefully. I'm actually as proud of the things we haven't done as the things I have done. Innovation is saying "no" to 1,000 things.

Tip 4: Determine which tasks are "urgent" and which ones are "important"

The productivity pioneer Stephen R. Covey popularized the time management matrix in his highly influential book "The 7 Habits of Highly Effective People." Here, he advised businesspeople to prioritize tasks by distinguishing between two dimensions: *importance* and *urgency*. There is a subtle difference between these two labels.

- An **important task** is a vital business activity that contributes to the fulfillment of your company mission, goals, or values.
- An **urgent task** is a business activity that requires your immediate attention. But the successful completion of the task may not necessarily advance your long-term objectives.

To properly taxonomize our daily tasks, Covey advised that we create four categories. Each task receives a label of:

- Not Important and Not Urgent

- Not Important but Urgent
- Important but Not Urgent
- Important and Urgent

Let's take a moment to understand each category.

- **Not Important and Not Urgent** tasks are the easiest to avoid doing. Since they're labeled "not important," they do not play a critical role in achieving your long-term goals. And since they're "not urgent," they do not require immediate attention. These activities often manifest as *distractions* and mostly only succeed in drawing the leader's attention away from her most vital objectives.
- **Not Important but Urgent** tasks are those that demand your immediate attention but do not contribute to your long-term goals. These tasks can be deceptive in their ploy to rob you of your precious time because they may appear out of nowhere, often in the form of a chirping text message, a whining employee, or the digital cry of a printer that's out of ink. It's quite easy to be fooled by such shrill alarms. But an astute businessperson can recognize them for what they are: *time-robbing distractions*.
- **Important but Not Urgent** tasks are activities that play a crucial role in achieving your long-term business objectives. But they don't necessarily call upon you to engage in immediate action. Instead, such tasks can be attended to as you would the slow burn of a hot fire. Activities in this domain might include strategic planning, relationship-building, and professional development.
- **Important and Urgent** tasks are activities that are critical to your long-term success and require your immediate attention. These tasks are non-negotiable. They need to be

addressed swiftly and promptly, often requiring your personal expertise and authority to complete. Examples of such tasks might include crisis management, urgent client requests, or dealing with a critical system breakdown. Neglecting such situations could lead to immediate and long-lasting consequences for your company.

Covey's matrix is so useful because it forces us to develop a keen sense of discernment. We are asked to continuously evaluate each task, ensuring that we're not just reacting to every demand that comes across our desk, but rather acting in a way that aligns with our most pivotal goals. The battlefield on which every leader must walk is a chaotic one. Endless challenges and opportunities can be found on your left and right flanks. Each foxhole is host to a unique set of obstacles. Each hilltop reveals a vista of prospects. But as you traverse the battlefield, it is crucial to remember that not every foxhole is worth exploring, and not every hilltop needs to be conquered. Some foxholes are mere distractions. And some hilltops are not worth the climb.

The ability to focus one's mind on the objectives that *truly* matter—to differentiate between the *vital* and the *trivial*—is one of the most difficult skills a boss can learn. The goal of *personal productivity* is to get the most mileage from your mind and body each day, all without damaging your health and psyche. As Greg McKeown (author of "Essentialism: The Disciplined Pursuit of Less") wrote:

Productivity is not about how to get more things done; it's about how to get the right things done. It doesn't mean just doing less for the sake of less... [It's] about making the wisest possible investment of

your time and energy in order to operate at [your] highest point of contribution.

Conclusion

In this book, we have delved deep into the intricacies of the female leadership role. And we have attempted to enumerate the many nuanced differences that distinguish a mere office manager from an *inspiring leader*. Along this trek, we've gathered many tools that should be of use to you on your journey.

- We discussed Daniel Goleman's five components of leadership (self-awareness, self-regulation, social skill, empathy, and motivation), and we explained how the boss can utilize *emotional intelligence* to help foster an environment of trust and collaboration in the workspace.
- We reviewed the six leadership styles (commanding, pacesetting, democratic, affiliative, coaching, and visionary), and discussed the importance of adopting an agile stance when deciding which mode of communication is best suited to your current situation.
- We described how you can use a *SWOT Analysis* (of your Strengths, Weaknesses, Opportunities, and Threats) to discover your company's *core competencies*. And how *SMART Goals* can be utilized to streamline your strategic planning efforts.
- We discussed the importance of assembling a team of devoted employees, and described how we might use *Tuckman's Ladder* to evaluate the group dynamics at play as your team traverses each stage of a lengthy project.

- We dived deep into the chambers of the mind, revealing such subtle psychological topics as imposter syndrome, empathy, conscientiousness, self-doubt, and feminine energy.
- Finally, we described how every boss must contend with the threat of *burnout*. And we enumerated the importance of achieving a viable work-life balance, which is essential to maintaining your health, vitality, and productivity.

I hope I was able to convince you of the immense value to be had when each one of these tools is successfully integrated into your leadership toolbox. The trick to becoming both a great boss and a great leader lies in mastering the practical aspects of management, while intuiting and molding the subtle psychological forces that are unique to every workplace. As is the case with so many other aspects of our life, leadership is a game of brinkmanship.

- We must devote resources to the achievement of our collective goal, while still heeding to the individual needs of each team member.
- We must strategize for the future, while remaining attuned to the present challenges that await us at the office each morning.
- We must be resolute in our decisions, yet remain open to feedback.
- We must be firm, but compassionate.
- We must keep our eyes on the stars but remain grounded in reality.

Your ability to embrace this delicate equilibrium will (in large part) influence both the velocity and the means by which your vision is achieved. As women, we possess an innate ability to balance such dichotomies. We are natural peacemakers, able to finesse complex political situations with empathy and grace. Such a nuanced skillset is essential for cultivating unity within a diverse set of employees, who can only complete a complex endeavor if they work in harmony. It is the leader's job to manage such divergent interests, all while ensuring that the overarching goal of the organization is attained with efficiency and group cohesion.

Ideally, we want our workforce to function like a well-oiled machine. One in which all the interconnected gears spin in harmony—complementing each other's strengths and compensating for each other's weaknesses, outputting a stream of viable products in a manner so fluid that few would be able to guess at the complexity of the underlying machinery. We don't have a word that adequately describes this phenomenon in English. However, such a marvel is perhaps more aptly conveyed by the Italian word "sprezzatura." The word first appeared in a 16th-century book by the Italian diplomat Baldassare Castiglione who defined it this way:

Sprezzatura means to possess a certain nonchalance … to make whatever one does or say appear to be without effort and almost without any thought about it. [The practitioner manifests] an easy facility in accomplishing difficult actions which hides the conscious effort that went into them.

The Oxford Dictionary simply defines it as "studied carelessness." But perhaps the closest English expression that captures the spirit of the word is:

Everything went off without a hitch.

Meaning that the function you were organizing (be that a wedding or a product launch) was executed in such a manner that each of the participants benefited from the effort, and no one suspected the amount of forethought that went into its creation.

As a business leader, this is exactly how you'd like each workday to go. When an organization is set up to function properly, your staff won't need to be prodded to action like military cadets. Instead, they'll all be busily engaged in their own assigned endeavors, working diligently without any knowledge of the underlying machinations that were carefully devoted to arranging the workspace. Hopefully, after reading this book, you are in a better position to create such a productive environment, where leadership feels effortless, employee motivations are aligned with the company's vision, and the organization thrives as a unified entity.

Of course, I should emphasize that the preceding description is merely a sketch of what an ideal company would look like. In actuality, many of your workdays will be filled with grueling challenges, befuddling moments of self-doubt, and unexpected hurdles brought about by the inevitable vicissitudes of the business landscape. For each mile you traverse, life will be ever willing to introduce new and increasingly diverse obstacles into your path. All you can do is lean into the journey—your mind ready for each battle with the forces of entropy, your eyes cast forward, forever scanning the horizon in search of serendipity.

Leaders are tasked with holding the torch and finding the path forward, even when the terrain is shrouded with uncertainty and laden with obscure obstacles. By remaining resilient during each daily catastrophe, your observed behaviors will cultivate a culture of tenacity, inspiring your team to remain steadfast and unified in the face of adversity, even when you're no longer there to light the way. As the former Facebook COO Sheryl Sandberg wrote:

Leadership is about making others better as a result of your presence, and making sure that impact lasts in your absence.

As women in leadership positions, the actions we take and the behaviors we manifest will sometimes be scrutinized with greater intensity. But such disparities must not be perceived as a reason to abandon our cause. Instead, we owe it to the upcoming generation of young women to challenge such biases, forever striving to defeat stereotypes via the merit of our work and the strength of our character.

I hope the insights and tools presented here will aid you on your leadership journey. This book has been a dream of mine ever since I entered the business world. May it serve as just one beacon of many—a faint light cast about a galaxy of bright stars, each one bearing the name of a firebrand of the feminist movement. Many points of light guide your way; so go forth with confidence and passion. For the first time in the history of our species, the talents within us have been uncaged. Use them to shape a brighter future and a more inclusive tomorrow. Use them well.

Here's to strong women everywhere.

"May we know them. May we raise them. May we be them."

Did you like the book?

Thank you for coming along for the ride with me. I really hope you enjoyed the book. If so, then please consider writing a book review. For an independent author like me, book reviews mean *everything*, and I personally read each one.

Or, if you have any suggestions on how I can improve my next book, don't be shy about contacting me. I look forward to hearing from you!

Thanks again,

Serena

Printed in Great Britain
by Amazon

59404080R00077